THE
ISLE OF WIGHT

by Brian Dicks

DAVID & CHARLES

NEWTON ABBOT LONDON NORTH POMFRET (Vt)

To Anne, Jean, Molly and Brian,
without whose help . . .

British Library Cataloguing in Publication Data

Dicks, Brian
   The Isle of Wight. – (The Islands series).
1. Wight, Isle of – History
I. Title II. Series
942.2'8   DA670.W6

ISBN 0 7153 7657 8

   Library of Congress Catalog Card Number 78–74082

Set by Northern Phototypesetting Co Bolton
and printed in Great Britain
by Biddles Limited Guildford
for David & Charles (Publishers) Limited
Brunel House Newton Abbot Devon

Published in the United States of America
by David & Charles Inc
North Pomfret Vermont 05053 USA

CONTENTS

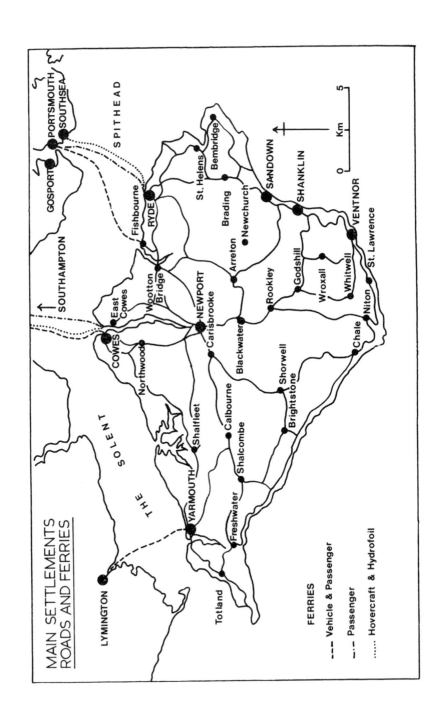

MAIN SETTLEMENTS
ROADS AND FERRIES

SPITHEAD

PORTSMOUTH/SOUTHSEA
GOSPORT

SOUTHAMPTON

THE SOLENT

LYMINGTON

Totland

Freshwater

YARMOUTH

Shalcombe

Calbourne

Shalfleet

Northwood

COWES
East Cowes

Wootton Bridge

Fishbourne

RYDE

St. Helens

Bembridge

Brading

Newchurch

SANDOWN

SHANKLIN

NEWPORT

Carisbrooke

Arreton

Blackwater

Rookley

Godshill

Wroxall

Whitwell

VENTNOR

St. Lawrence

Niton

Chale

Shorwell

Brightstone

Ferries

--- Vehicle & Passenger

-..- Passenger

.... Hovercraft & Hydrofoil

0   Km   5

1   CROSSING THE BAR

Sunset and evening star,
And one clear call for me!
And may there be no moaning of the bar,
When I put out to sea.

Alfred Lord Tennyson

THESE lines are the first in a short four stanza poem which, on its published appearance in 1889, created as profound an impression as any other work in the English language. The valedictory *Crossing the Bar* came to Tennyson on an evening in October in his eighty-first year when making the homeward passage between Lymington in Hampshire and the small port of Yarmouth on the western coast of the Isle of Wight. The journey across The Solent was one he had made many times before, but on this occasion the sight of an outward-bound steamer dropping its pilot in the twilight near The Needles prompted the lyric which came to be held as a worthy crown to his long career of literary achievement.

The 'bar' in question might have referred to the sandbank across the harbour mouth where the winding course of the Lymington or Boldre River enters The Solent, or perhaps Tennyson had in mind the protective sea barrier that surrounds the island and separates it from the coast of Hampshire. In its real sense, of course, the poem was allegorical and alluded to Tennyson's own death, with the 'call', a maritime term for a summons to duty suggestive of this, as was the 'pilot' symbolising God, in the last stanza. *Crossing the Bar* was jotted down on the inside of a used envelope and that evening Tennyson showed it to his eldest son, Hallam, who recognised it as a fitting finale to his father's life's work.

. Though not a native of the Isle of Wight, Tennyson loved it with an islander's passion and drew great inspiration from the beauty, variety and interest of its landscape. He was a naturalist in the broadest sense, a careful student, as well as an observer of nature, whose moods and seasons gave him so many of his felicitous comparisons and most striking lines. Yet, above all, it was the island's seclusion and solitude that attracted Tennyson and finally persuaded him to settle, in 1853, at Farringford, a large, basically eighteenth-century house near Freshwater.

Communications to West Wight at this time were still difficult for the mainland trains came no nearer than Brockenhurst in the New Forest, whence travellers proceeded by horse-drawn bus to Lymington pier to catch the steamer. When the bus was delayed, as was often the case, the crossing to Yarmouth was made by rowing boat and the remainder of the journey to Farringford in a donkey cart. It is reported that, on arrival, the two maids who had accompanied Tennyson, his wife and son, burst into tears, exclaiming that they would never be able to endure such loneliness. For the poet, however, Farringford was situated amongst some of the island's finest scenery where 'far from noise and smoke of town', as he described his existence in 1854 in a poetic invitation to the Rev F. D. Maurice, Tennyson was able, at least initially, to walk undisturbed over downs, valleys and beaches.

Though one of the Isle of Wight's most illustrious characters, Tennyson was not the only poet or writer to seek inspiration from its shores. When John Keats visited the island in 1817 and 1819 The Solent and Spithead crossings were more difficult propositions with sailing ships sometimes taking up to four hours to reach Ryde from Portsmouth. With a favourable wind the journey could be accomplished in an hour, but, equally, there were many days when weather conditions precluded all contact between island and mainland. For Keats, with his romantic inclinations, however, such inconvenience was more than compensated for by the island's wealth of natural beauty which he praised in a persuasive letter to his friend, John Reynolds, inviting him to visit Carisbrooke. Perhaps it is no coincidence that the opening lines of *Endymion* which Keats was writing at this time, are now among the best known in English literature: 'A thing of beauty is a joy for ever, its loveliness increases, it will never pass into nothingness.' This was probably read to Reynolds on his arrival at Carisbrooke.

For the whole of July and August 1819 Keats stayed at Shanklin. Here he wrote *Lamia* and *Otho the Great* and again in a number of letters he enthusiastically praises his surroundings. 'Shanklin', he wrote to Reynolds, 'is a beautiful place—sloping wood and meadow ground reaches the chine which is a cleft between the cliffs of the depth of nearly three hundred feet at least. This cleft is filled with trees and bushes in the narrow parts; and as it widens becomes bare, if it were not for primroses on one side, which spread to the very edge of the sea, and some fishermen's huts on the other, perched midway in the balustrades of beautiful green hedges along their steps down to the sands.' The chine and other natural curiosities became a favourite study for the nineteenth-century painters and engravers who loved to romanticise and overdramatise such locations. Of these, George Brannon, an Irishman by birth, is perhaps the most famous producing, between 1821 and 1857, over 170 illustrations for his *Vectis Scenery*.

'Leafy Shanklin', as Keats described it, also had other admirers. To Longfellow on his visit to England in 1868 it was 'one of the quietest and loveliest places in the kingdom' and he was moved to leave six sentimental lines, though some say they were his finest, on a fountain amongst its old thatched cottages. Longfellow's feelings were echoed in 1880 by those of the French writer, Paul Bourget, who on leaving Shanklin and the island was comforted by memories of 'beautiful green lawns, cold blue seas and delicately grey skies'.

Yet of all the literary corners of nineteenth-century Wight, and indeed England, the village of Bonchurch, for its size, must rank as supreme. A parish when Ventnor was a few cottages, Bonchurch by the end of the nineteenth century was a suburb of the town, but one where the praises of its former personalities still applied. Here Swinburne spent his childhood and lies buried in the nineteenth-century churchyard, as does de Vere Stacpoole. Its roll call of other notables includes Tennyson before he settled at Freshwater, Macaulay who resided at Madeira Hall, Anna Sewell of *Black Beauty* fame and Dickens, who began *Great Expectations* in Bonchurch and claimed that 'from the top of the highest down there are views which are only to be equalled on the Genoese shore of the Mediterranean'.

The Isle of Wight's praises were certainly sung during the nineteenth century, but these literary giants who visited, seasoned and settled, were just part of a greater movement which turned the island into a garden resort for the Victorian upper and middle classes. The factors collectively involved in this process are discussed in a later chapter, but the ultimate results were the converse of the very things that had initially attracted the poets and writers. By the end of the century improved communications with the mainland and within the island led to the establishment of a more democratic holiday industry and an ever-increasing number of Victorians 'crossed the bar'. Seclusion was broken down, solitude disrupted and to Tennyson, in particular, this proved intolerable.

The fame and success of Tennyson, especially with poems such as *Maud*, had already turned Farringford and Freshwater into an important Victorian centre of culture and a place of pilgrimage. Farringford received and entertained celebrated personalities from all branches of literature, music, philosophy and science, not to mention royalty and secular heads of state. 'Everybody at Freshwater', wrote Anne Thackeray, the daughter of the novelist, 'is either a genius, or a poet, or a painter, or peculiar in some way.' It was not eccentricity, however, that disturbed Tennyson but the number of prying sightseers who even invaded the grounds of

CROSSING THE BAR

Farringford to catch sight of the Poet Laureate who was known
to stride along the lanes and downs, clad in wide-brimmed hat,
long black cloak and muttering to himself. Tennyson in fact
had often turned back from a favourite walk, probably over the
nearby downs, because he had mistaken a flock of sheep for a
herd of trippers. The publication date of *Crossing the Bar* had
coincided with the extension of the island's railway network
from Newport, via Yarmouth, to Freshwater. This made the
poet's life intolerable. He died, three years later, not at
Farringford but at his Sussex home. A few days before his death
he had requested that *Crossing the Bar* be put at the end of all
editions of his works, a fitting tribute to the Isle of Wight and
the scenic beauties he immortalised.

The Solent and Spithead are crossed today by regular ferry
services linking island ports with mainland destinations which
have train connections with London and elsewhere. The 25–30
minute passage between Lymington and Yarmouth is
normally worked by British Rail Sealink ferries MV *Cenwulf,
Cenred* and *Freshwater* which are combined passenger-car
vessels. The same company operates the popular passenger
ferry between Portsmouth Harbour and Ryde (25 minute
crossing) and the car ferry service from Portsmouth to
Fishbourne (MV *Cuthred, Caedmon, Fishbourne* and *Camber
Queen*). Red Funnel Services operate combined passenger and
car ferries between Southampton and Cowes and the journey
time in vessels such as *Cowes Castle* and *Netley Castle* (the largest
cross-Solent ferry) is 50 minutes. In addition to these efficient,
but more leisurely boat trips, there are hovercraft services from
Southampton to Cowes (20 minutes), from Southsea to Ryde
(7 minutes) and the Red Funnel Hydrofoil from Southampton
to Cowes (20 minutes). These services now mean that London
can be reached from Cowes in 1 hour 50 minutes.

What travellers expect to find after 'crossing the bar' by
these modern methods depends, of course, on their own
inclinations and pre-conceived ideas of the Isle of Wight. Many
will undoubtedly be initially surprised, perhaps even

11

disappointed, not by the present beauties of land and sea, nor by the character and courtesy of its inhabitants, but by the fact that the island looks remarkably similar to parts of the south coast and its cliché description as 'a miniature England' might seem justified. Functionally, too, there is little that immediately distinguishes it from the mainland: it has many of the ubiquitous chain stores (though population threshold size precludes others); the mainland breweries have carved out their island territories; the bus company, though called 'Vectis' (the Roman name for the island), is part of the National group; its railways have suffered the same Beeching fate as those in other parts of the country; there is no Isle of Wight bank or currency as in the Channel Islands; its local accent (in spite of a dictionary of Isle of Wight dialect published in the 1880s) is no more incomprehensible than 'deep' Devonian, Yorkshire or East Anglian; it has no special postage stamps and, unlike the Isle of Man, its laws are identical to those of England and Wales.

The question remains, therefore: is there anything that makes the Isle of Wight different? This could be answered in a non-committal way by stating that its only peculiarity is the geographical fact that it is an island and insularity, of necessity, brings its own attendant problems, advantages and attitudes to life. Yet on the positive side there is the firm historical fact that the Isle of Wight was not incorporated into the English realm until the end of the thirteenth century, and as a mark of this anomaly it still has its Governor, an honorary title today, but a position which is appointed by the Crown and continues the earlier and more powerful distinctions of Lord or Captain of the island. The fact is that on the Isle of Wight there has never been any serious opposition, manifest or latent, to conformity with the broad, general pattern of English life, if anything, it has been the reverse for the island has always been strongly patriotic and royalist and is proud of its strong associations with the Crown.

Yet conformity in this sense should not detract from the fact that the Isle of Wight has retained, woven into the general

English pattern, a way and attitude to life that is very much its own. Its people not merely consider themselves as islanders but as people of *the* island, not just separate, but different from the mainlanders whom they call 'overners'. This is not a disparaging adjective and has not the implications of the semi-national Cornish term 'emmet', used for everyone east of Bodmin or at least the Tamar. The Vectensians realise that at one time they were all 'overners', for Celts, Romans, Saxons, perhaps Jutes, Normans and less defined strains of later centuries have combined to mould the present islander's character. Their attitude to the annual influx of pleasure-seeking 'overners' is also intelligent and one which recognises the fact that the island's economy is today dependent on these trans-Solent migrants.

The Isle of Wight is attractive at all times of year, but it displays its greatest charms out of season when the scenes and characters of its past appear in their true light to colour and enrich the fabric of the present.

2   THE ISLAND ENVIRONMENT

That beautiful island which he who once
sees never forgets through whatever part
of the world his future may lead him.

Sir Walter Scott

ALTHOUGH Victorian romanticism, local magniloquence and lucid descriptions in holiday brochures have all tended to exaggerate its claim, it is not without some justification that the Isle of Wight calls itself England's 'garden isle'. In spite of its small area the island's varied geological structure, diverse topography and rich natural vegetation, modified by agriculture, have collectively produced some of southern England's most attractive and unspoiled countryside. Its scenic assets are important factors in its popularity as a holiday centre and today about half of the island's area is designated as being of outstanding natural beauty and landscape value, as defined by the Council for the Protection of Rural England. This area includes 38 miles (59km) of coastline, a major aspect of the island scene, whose character varies from precipitous chalk cliffs to flat, marshy estuaries or sand and shingle beaches. Together with National Trust properties, nature reserves, long distance trails, coastal paths and areas of special scientific interest as notified by the Nature Conservancy, a large part of the island is thus protected or overseered by national bodies and local organisations such as the Isle of Wight Natural History and Archaeological Society.

The attractiveness of the island, however, is not just a

function of geology, topography and vegetation. Its landscape and scenery are as much the products of human or cultural forces, and the island is particularly fortunate in having areas of great scenic value which are the results of agricultural management and its attendant land use and settlement patterns. Fields, farms, hedges, manors, copses, villages, mills and churches are integral elements in the island's composite character revealing centuries of growth, evolution and adaptation to local environmental conditions. The various stages in the island's historical development are discussed in subsequent chapters but they were enacted in an island setting whose physical character was the product of an eventful geological and erosional history.

THE SOLENT RIVER

Wight was not always an island. Until well after the last Ice Age it was physically joined to what is now the Hampshire coast, and its separation was the result of post-glacial changes in sea levels and the consequent marine breaching of a continuous chalk barrier of which the Purbeck downs and the island's central spinal ridge are surviving sections (see map). These are now separated by a sea gap of nearly twenty miles (32km) with the Old Harry Rocks and The Needles as their respective outlying fragments. This chalk barrier completed the

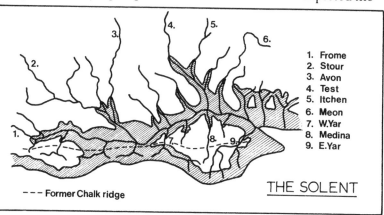

1. Frome
2. Stour
3. Avon
4. Test
5. Itchen
6. Meon
7. W.Yar
8. Medina
9. E.Yar

- - - Former Chalk ridge

THE SOLENT

15

southern side of the Hampshire syncline and protected an area of low-lying Tertiary deposits, now submerged as Bournemouth Bay, against wave attack and other forms of erosion.

The basin was drained eastwards by the so-called 'Solent river' which may be regarded as a southern counterpart of the Thames. It was fed by many sizeable tributaries, the most distant now lying within the borders of modern Somerset. From the north the 'Solent' received the ancestors of rivers such as the Test, Stour, Avon and Itchen, whilst its tributaries from the south were the now diminutive Isle of Wight rivers whose courses, on account of land lying south of its present shores, were then more extensive. Today the old course of the 'Solent river' is represented by the Dorset Frome and by The Solent and Spithead straits.

The chronology of the final breakthrough of the Chalk ridge is still a matter of controversy. Britain became physically detached from the European continent somewhere around 6000–7000 BC and though some authorities place the event much later, it is highly probable that the Isle of Wight received its own insularity about the same time. The date is of geological significance only, for the outcome was the same—the creation of what came to be a diamond-shaped island of some 155 square miles (397 sq km) with a maximum length of 23 miles (35km) from The Needles in the west to Bembridge Foreland in the east, and a maximum width of 13 miles (21km) from Egypt Point at Cowes to St Catherine's Point in the south.

The Solent and Spithead, which separate it from the Hampshire coast, meet at Cowes Road to form the deep inlet leading to Southampton Water up which the world's largest ships can readily proceed. The shelter afforded by the Isle of Wight played an important part in the development of this historic waterway, but contrary to popular belief it is not responsible for the freak bonus of double tides which have made Southampton and Portsmouth the maritime centres they are. The tides, which also affect the island ports of Yarmouth, Cowes and, to a lesser extent, Newport, are the result of up-

Shanklin Chine – one of the island's natural curiosities which Victorian artists
and writers loved to romanticise *(British Tourist Authority)*

One of the most famous of British landmarks for shipping, the Needles are a classic textbook example of the effects of marine erosion on chalk *(British Tourist Authority)*

channel tidal surges meeting those coming down-channel from the North Sea. The Venerable Bede almost had it right. 'In this sea', he states, 'comes a double tide out of the seas which spring from the infinite ocean of the Arctic which surrounds all Britain.'

GEOLOGY AND SCENERY

In 1921, in the preface to *A Short Account of the Geology of the Isle of Wight*, the Director of the Geological Survey commented that 'no district of England of comparative size is more interesting to the geologist than the Isle of Wight, alike from the variety of its formations, the excellence of its exposures and the abundance of fossils'. Others have commented that the island 'might have been cut out by nature for a geological model illustrative of the phenomena of stratification'. Certainly, since the mid-nineteenth century, it has been investigated in detail by professionals and amateurs, especially its coasts whose exposures, due to active erosion, vary in detail from year to year.

In common with southern England generally the island is composed entirely of sedimentary rocks and its succession extends from the Lower Cretaceous Wealden Marls to the highest British Oligocene rocks, the Hampstead Beds. This is a stratigraphical sequence of eighteen major formations with numerous sub-divisions or facies within them. Thus, in a comparatively small geographical area there is great lithological variety which is supplemented by Pleistocene and recent superficial deposits such as valley, plateau and flint gravels, together with blown sand, alluvium and peat.

The Wealden Beds are brought to the surface in Sandown Bay by the Sandown–Arreton anticline, part of the mid-Tertiary or Alpine series of earth movements responsible for a markedly asymmetrical fold structure across the centre of the island. This 'monocline' has dips approaching the vertical on the north but gentler inclinations and, hence, wider outcrops occur to the south. The Brighstone anticline is responsible for

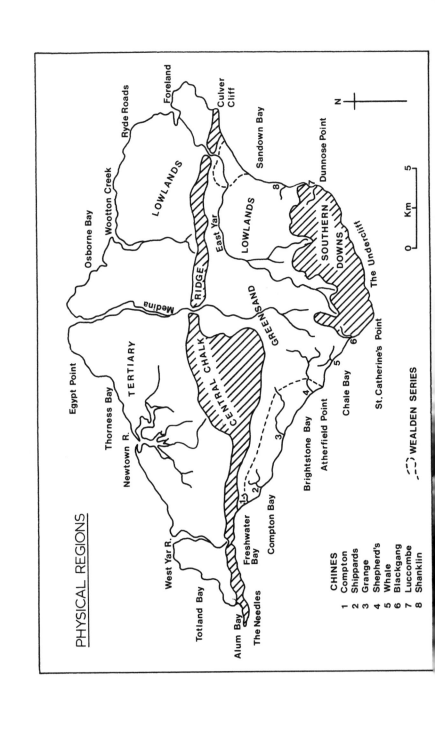

PHYSICAL REGIONS

Egypt Point
Thorness Bay
TERTIARY
Newtown R.
West Yar R.
Totland Bay
Alum Bay
The Needles
Freshwater Bay
Compton Bay
CENTRAL CHALK
Medina
RIDGE
LOWLANDS
Osborne Bay
Wootton Creek
Ryde Roads
Foreland
East Yar
Culver Cliff
Sandown Bay
LOWLANDS
GREENSAND
Brightstone Bay
Atherfield Point
Chale Bay
St. Catherine's Point
SOUTHERN DOWNS
The Undercliff
Dunnose Point

CHINES
1 Compton
2 Shippards
3 Grange
4 Shepherd's
5 Whale
6 Blackgang
7 Luccombe
8 Shanklin

WEALDEN SERIES

N

0   Km   5

further exposures of the Wealden Series along the south-west coast between Compton Bay and Atherfield Point. These beds are important not merely because they are the island's oldest but because they have yielded many fossil bones including a few almost complete skeletons of giant reptiles.

For the landscape student, however, the interest of the Isle of Wight lies in the way in which topography faithfully reflects geological structure. If generalisations can be made, then it is the porous, but resistant, chalk and associated beds that form the island's dominating relief features—dissected downlands and impressive cliffs—whilst the softer sands and clays produce gentler lowlands and rich farmlands. The great diversity in rock type adds tremendous local detail which is often reflected in vegetation and general land use patterns.

The Island's Spine
Although the island is fairly evenly divided by the Medina River which crosses it amost completely from north to south, nearly along the line of its greatest breadth, the most important topographical feature is the central chalk ridge of downland which extends from The Needles to Culver Cliff near Bembridge. It effectively divides the island into two broad areas of entirely different character and though rarely exceeding 450ft (150m), it stands out prominently above the clays, sands and other deposits which flank it. Broken at Newport by the Medina, at Brading by the Yar, and elsewhere, it carries a number of down names which derive from ancient parishes, medieval manors and, in the case of Tennyson Down, island notables.

For most of its length this Chalk ridge is narrow (from three-quarters to half a mile wide) for the beds dip steeply and are often almost vertical which means that the surface outcrop is not much more than its total thickness, that is, around 1,500ft (495m). Near the centre of the island, however, south and west of Newport, the dip is lower and the ridge expands to a small upland two to four miles wide, which at Brighstone Down attains its highest elevation of 700ft (231m), affording some of

21

the most extensive views on the island. Deeply dissected by a complex network of dry valleys, its thin soil supports the close turf characteristic of downland and is interspersed with patches of gorse and brambles. In the west between Freshwater Bay and The Needles, part of which is the National Trust property of Tennyson Down, similar downland features occur though without the dissection, but having the added attraction of an imposing coastal location.

The seaward terminations of the Chalk ridge give rise to imposing cliffs which at Scratchell's Bay in the west and Culver Cliff in the east rise to heights of nearly 400ft (132m). The elevation and general character of the cliffs depends on the dip or angle of inclination of the strata. Where the chalk dips steeply seawards, as on the north side of Culver headland and at Alum Bay, the cliff often approximates in angle to the bedding-planes and takes on a 'slabby' appearance; but where the dip is inland the bedding-planes are very sharply truncated and near-vertical cliffs may result. Lines of weakness are commonly etched into caves, arches and, ultimately, stacks. Those developed at The Needles are widely known, but other good examples occur such as the Arched Rock and the Stag Rock in Freshwater Bay which, though smaller in scale, are of similar origin.

The Needles are probably one of the most famous of British coastal features. They have been drawn, painted (on canvas) and photographed from every convenient angle and are classic textbook examples of the effects of marine erosion on Chalk. These five sea stacks, of which only three are conspicuous, fall into line with the island's main ridge and on a clear day the Chalk cliffs under Ballard Down, across Bournemouth Bay, may be seen continuing the alignment. Two engravings, dating from the middle of the eighteenth century, show a fourth prominent stack, a slender pinnacle about 120ft (40m) high, which fell in 1764 and which was probably responsible for the name of the group though it was called Lot's Wife. An arch joining the inner rock to the mainland collapsed about the time of the Battle of Waterloo.

The Northern Lowlands

The division between the Chalk ridge and the northern lowlands is geologically and topographically abrupt and can be followed at Alum Bay, north of The Needles headland. This is another of the island's coastal curiosities for a great thickness of Eocene Beds have been up-ended, almost vertically, by the Alpine earth movements. Twenty-nine different sorts of strata have been recognised, which were originally deposited in many varying conditions, in shallow seas and deep ones, salt water and brackish, and under many kinds of climate as revealed by the fossil record. The bay is particularly famous for its coloured sands and cliffs which comprise the Bagshot Sands and Bracklesham Beds. Twelve different shades of colour can be recognised which are seen at their best after rain.

At Alum Bay the almost vertical dip of the Eocene deposits contrasts greatly with the horizontal arrangement of the Headen Beds which are the lowest of the Oligocene clays, marls, and other deposits, which make up the northern part of the Isle of Wight. This geological unconformity can again be seen in the east of the island where Whitecliffe Bay, immediately north of Culver Cliff, occupies a similar position to Alum Bay. Above the Headen Beds are the 70–80ft (21–24m) thick Osborne Beds which, with the exception of a small outlier near Lyndhurst on the mainland, are confined to the Isle of Wight. In turn, they are succeeded by the Bembridge Limestone, the Bembridge Marl and the Lower and Upper Hampstead Beds which occur only in the west between Hampstead and Bouldnor.

Topographically the northern part of the Isle of Wight is irregular lowland country whose elevation varies between 100 and 180ft (33–60m). Its most prominent heights are related to superficial deposits of plateau gravels which cover considerable areas on either side of the Medina estuary, with smaller patches along the north-east and north-west coasts. In many places, as in the Parkhurst vicinity, these gravels produce small but regular hills which are of great value as observation or vantage points in an otherwise undulating countryside. Along the Spithead coast the soft rocks provide shelving shorelines and when low cliffs are present they are generally overgrown. The Bembridge Foreland, however, is composed of a more resistant limestone occurring within the Oligocene strata. The Solent coast is more varied and has cliffs at Gurnard and south of Newtown Bay, but large sections are the products of coastal accretion leading to the formation of extensive mud-flats and salt-marshes. The Newtown estuary, now National Trust property, is the largest and most interesting of these, but smaller examples occur.

The generally heavy and ill-drained soils of the northern lowlands support a large number of copses and woodlands, of which Parkhurst Forest is the most extensive. Pastoralism is the main land use but a more varied belt lies to the south where a narrow zone of mixed soils is the product of downwash processes from the chalk ridge.

The Bowl of the Island
Though again basically low-lying, the country to the south of the Chalk ridge shows greater scenic variation and presents, in every respect, a strong contrast to that of the north. Rocks belonging to the Lower Cretaceous Wealden and Lower Greensand series form a denuded belt which in effect is an anticlinal vale not unlike the more extensive structure of the Kent and Sussex Weald. It opens in a wide expanse of undulating lowland along the south-west coast from Brook to Chale and then narrows inland through Kingston and Chale Green to broaden again eastwards into an almost rectangular area of poorly drained countryside which reaches the coast at Sandown Bay.

This part of the island is difficult to characterise but its fertile soils, cultivated fields, wooded ridges, rich green pastures and local topographical detail combine to make it one of the most interesting areas.

The Southern Downs
The anticlinal structure of the southern part of the island

means that the Chalk downland again appears between Chale and Shanklin though it has been much eroded to expose the underlying Upper Greensand and Gault Clay. Here, however, the Isle of Wight reaches its highest elevations in St Catherine's Down (779ft, 236m), Shanklin Down (779ft, 236m) and St Boniface Down (776ft, 235m). Like the central Chalk ridge and counterparts in southern and eastern England, these southern Downs are highly dissected by a system of valleys which, although the products of surface run off, contain no permanent and, in some cases, no temporary streams.

The origin of dry valleys remains a debatable issue though undoubtedly they are partly the result of a fall in the level of the water table consequent on a steady decline in elevation of the scarp-foot springs. Basic to their understanding, however, are the periods of more humid climate and more surface run off in interglacial and postglacial times which accelerated stream erosion. There is also reason to believe that these valleys were partly moulded by periglacial processes such as frost attack and rapid freeze-thaw solifluction in Pleistocene times.

The Undercliff
Whereas the Southern Downs are deeply indented by valleys on their northern side, along the coast from Chale to Shanklin they form steep, often well-wooded slopes, much disturbed by landslides. Here, the combination of water percolating through strata, a pronounced seaward dip of rocks, and marine erosion have produced the beautiful, often romantic but dangerous scenery of the Undercliff. Porous Chalk and Upper Greensand overlie the Gault Clay, or the 'Blue Slipper' as it is known locally, with the result that water passing through the porous beds is held at the top of the clays, giving rise to a line of cliff springs and keeping the clay surface constantly lubricated. As these rocks have a gentle southerly dip there is a natural tendency for them to move seawards, often with disastrous results.

The jumbled mass of debris from St Catherine's Point to near Ventnor is the product of this slumping and sliding. It is under half-a-mile wide but is backed by inland cliffs some 200ft (66m) high. Further to the east a major landslip occurred between Luccombe Chine and Dunnose Point in 1818, producing an extensive area of natural debris where subsequent movements have caused repeated damage to the coastal road and to settlements. In 1951, for example, several houses were destroyed at Luccombe and in 1960 a number of buildings in Ventnor and adjacent St Lawrence were severely damaged. The danger of landslides is always increased with exceptional rainfall and it is not just confined to the coast for masses of Greensand have slipped down on all sides of St Catherine's Down.

THE WIGHT RIVERS

The drainage of the Isle of Wight, like its geology and scenery, presents many features of extraordinary interest. All of its important rivers and streams rise close to the south coast, yet flow northwards to the Solent and Spithead after cutting gaps through the Chalk ridge. In geomorphological terms the West Yar, the Medina and the East Yar are dip streams, but the positions of their sources are remarkable. The West Yar, for example, rises close to the coast at Freshwater Bay where the upper part of its valley cuts deeply into the landward side of the cliffs. River gravels, however, deposited by the Yar, are found right on the south coast and extend to The Solent, suggesting that the river which cut this valley must have, at one time, been considerably longer with its headwaters rising some distance to the south of the present shoreline (map, p 15). Modern cliff formations are indicative of the force of marine destruction along this part of the coast and the erosion of land obviously occurred subsequent to the rivers having carved their valleys. Today, the total fall of the West Yar between source and mouth is less than 20ft (6·6m) in a distance of 2·5 miles (3·4km). North of Freshwater it enters a wide ria estuary and only a slight depression of land, or rise in sea level, would make this western corner of Wight a separate island.

The island's main river, the Medina, follows a similar course pattern to the West Yar though it has not been beheaded as a result of marine erosion. It rises at the base of St Catherine's Down close to the southern coast and its regular northward course to The Solent traditionally divides the island into West and East Medina. To the north of Newport where the river is tidal, the Medina widens considerably to about one quarter of a mile at Cowes. The East Yar also originates in the vicinity of St Catherine's Down, but follows an irregular north-easterly course, receiving a number of southerly tributaries, to the drowned estuary which is now Bembridge Harbour. An extensive area of marshland extends inland to Brading, once an important harbour, through which the Yar has been canalised. Like its western counterpart the East Yar has lost much of its drainage area to sea encroachment and a small tributary with extensive alluvial deposits to the north-east of Sandown shows evidence of recent marine truncation.

Between the West Yar and the Medina an irregular finger-like series of inlets form the estuary of the Newtown River which, like the Yar at Brading, was once an important harbour until silting brought about its decline. The only other major stream on the island is Blackbridge Brook which rises at the base of Mersley Down and enters Spithead at Wootton Creek, the terminus of the Portsmouth car ferry.

The Chines

Although an essentially northern drainage dominates the Isle of Wight there are a number of small streams that descend rapidly to the sea from the higher ground near the south coast. Their steep gradients have produced ravine-like cuttings or chines, the products of severe cliff erosion leading to stream rejuvenation. The word chine is derived from the Anglo-Saxon *cine*, a chink or fissure, but their actual character is very much dependent on the rocks through which they are cut. Shanklin chine is a narrow winding cleft in the Greensand beds some 180ft (60m) wide on average and nearly 300ft (99m) deep. Its erosion is caused by the spring which rises close to its old church and in wet weather a cascade is formed, though at other times the stream is insignificant. The action of this water on the soft outcrops has, in the course of time, excavated this winding glen which is today clothed with thick undergrowth, tapering trees and prolific ferns. The chine widens towards the sea and from a few yards at its source it reaches 300ft (99m) at its mouth.

The character of Blackgang chine is completely different from that of Shanklin. Its sides are not as steep and its course not as winding, but it is of much greater depth with one of its flanks rising to over 400ft (132m) above sea level. The chine is little vegetated and its sides, composed chiefly of dark blue Gault Clay laced with layers of yellow sandstone, are continually crumbling.

Luccombe chine is another wild and impressive feature, and further west are the less spectacular Whale, Shepherd's, Grange, Chilton, Shippards, Compton and Brambles chines, all the products of stream erosion.

FAUNA AND FLORA

Ecological interest in the Isle of Wight is stimulated by the wide range of natural habitats, themselves a reflection of the island's variety in geological, topographical and soil conditions. Chalk downlands and patches of mixed woodlands contrast with more open heathland, rich valley floors and water meadows. The freshwater habitats are also varied with areas of bog which are somewhat acid in content contrasting sharply with the small streams on the Chalk. Estuaries are bordered in places by salt-marshes and the coastline itself lends further variety with shingle, mudflats, sandy beaches, prominent cliffs and rocky forelands. The attendant fauna and flora which accompany such a diversity are extremely rich and the close succession of geological outcrops can often be inferred from a careful observation of surface vegetation. Between Newtown and Porchfield, for example, elm and oak woods give way to hazel and hawthorn, the reason being a change in underlying soils as the Bembridge Marls emerge from underneath the Hampstead Beds.

Woodlands
Although the Isle of Wight is intensively settled and has been the home of man since prehistoric times, several tracts of natural, or semi-natural vegetation, particularly woodland, still survive. Oak and beech, with occasional stands of birchwood, ashwood and alder, occur as unexploited woodland and in parts of the north and on some areas of clay-with-flints overlying the Chalk, oakwood with hazel is characteristic. In the north and centre of the island, woodlands, together with copses and hedgerows, greatly contribute to the local scenery, whereas in the south, tree growth, because of coastal winds, is more restricted. Here, as throughout the island, stands of trees, and even individuals, are protected by tree preservation orders. From their natural state the island's woodlands have been much reduced, yet they still cover over 8,000 acres which is approximately 10 per cent of total area. Today, almost 65 per cent of this woodland is managed by the Forestry Commission which also advises on the care of trees not under its control. Modern forestry has introduced species which are not native to the island, such as the varied assemblage of conifers in Parkhurst Forest but these, together with hardwoods such as sycamore, maple and ash, add considerably to the local scenery. Parkhurst Forest was once Crown woodland and covers over 1,000 acres, but it is not as extensive as the Commission's reserve of Brighstone (1,350 acres), where on chalky soils a hardwood crop of beech is grown which in its young stage is protected by a nurse crop of Corsican pine.

The island's woodlands contain many interesting floral species. The woods of the clays and gravels of the north (as in parts of the New Forest) are characterised by a typically Hampshire plant, the Long-leaved Lungwort or 'Cowslips of Jerusalem'. Wild daffodils are found in many woods and a wide variety of other flowers. An interesting woodland area is the park around Fort Victoria, north of Totland. This has not been tended by man for at least thirty years and its vegetation shows all the stages of plant growth from simple mosses, lichens and ferns to deciduous tree species.

Downlands

Just as the natural woodlands of the island have been reduced, so through ploughing and afforestation, much of the natural downlands have disappeared. Isolated tracts still exist, as on Tennyson and Compton Downs, owned by the National Trust, and here the residual grassland slopes, with close springy turf, are rich in species. Typical plants include Dwarf Thistle, Wild Thyme, Horseshoe and Kidney Vetch, Rock Rose, Harebells, Sea Stock, Yellow Horned Poppy, Hairy Violet and Cowslips. Chalk, because of the extreme shallowness of its soil, produces stunted plants with short stems and small flowers, sometimes miniatures of larger editions growing elsewhere, but often only to be found on the Chalk. The ecology, however, is complex with local climatic factors playing an important role, for on Tennyson Down, the north facing side, away from the wind, and for much of the day in the shade, supports a totally different plant cover which includes holly, gorse, ivy, hawthorn and heather. Such species are also encouraged where the superficial deposits of clay-with-flints give acid soil conditions. Downland flora is dependent on the continued grazing by rabbits and sheep and the widespread reduction of the former by myxomatosis affected the character of the vegetation.

Heaths and Marshes

The island's heaths are confined to the poorer, often acid and infertile sands and gravels, and in depressions and valley bottoms where drainage is impeded, they tend to become boggy. Such conditions occur along the upper and middle courses of the Medina, especially south of Rookley in the area called The Wilderness, and also along wide sections of the East Yar where the surroundings of Horringford, Newchurch and Alverstone are particularly attractive botanical hunting grounds. The tidal marshes also provide distinctive plant associations of which Newtown River and its Nature Reserve is of great scientific significance. Here an area of 300 acres, representing a completely natural tidal estuarine habitat, has over 300 species of plant life, not to mention a wealth of marine creatures and bird life.

Mammals

The British mammal fauna is exceptionally well represented in the Isle of Wight. The fox, especially introduced for hunting purposes, is now common throughout the island, as are the badger, the stoat, and the weasel. Many of the small herbivorous mammals, if infrequently seen, by reason of their nocturnal habits, also have numerous representatives and include voles, shrews, dormice, hedgehogs, and moles. Otters occur, but only by the larger island streams and rivers. Perhaps the most significant animal, demonstrating the protective role of insularity, is the red squirrel. Although native to British woodlands it has largely been ousted from the mainland by the ubiquitous American grey squirrel. The latter species has not been introduced to the Isle of Wight. Rabbits are very common and the brown hare is widespread.

Of the marine mammals, the porpoise and the dolphin have been found stranded along the island's coast, and the common seal is not an unknown visitor.

Reptiles and Amphibia

The six British species of reptiles are present in the Isle of Wight. The viper or adder, grass snake, common lizard and slow worm are widespread, but the sand lizard and smooth snake have more localised habitats. The toad, frog, crested and smooth newt are abundant.

Bird life

For the ornithologist the woodlands, salt-marshes, downlands and cliffs provide a wealth of environments for the island's bird life. Sea birds are naturally plentiful and large colonies are found on the cliffs of the south-west. The nesting species include cormorant, shag, guillemot, razorbill, puffin, herring gull, great black-backed gull, kittiwake and sometimes fulmar.

Culver Cliff is another important area for bird life and formerly a characteristic species was the peregrine, which, in the heyday of falconry, was prized for its prowess. In 1554, a warrant was issued for the arrest of persons stealing young birds which were the property of the Crown. Peregrines have seriously declined in Britain and they are now seldom seen in the Isle of Wight.

The name Culver might originate from 'gulvre' or 'culppe', a Saxon name meaning pigeon and referring to the number of rock doves that once nested on the cliff face. White-tailed eagles also once inhabited Culver Cliff and a nest reported in 1780 may have been the last in England.

The marshland area to the south and east of Brading is unique in terms of its bird life for it is the feeding area for many wading species and wildfowl. This is a freshwater march and common birds include shelduck, redshank, mallard, reed bunting, reed warbler and sedge warbler. Other wading birds, such as the oyster-catcher, ringed plover, dunlin, and curlew, can be seen at Thorness Bay. The Newtown Reserve is important for its salt-marsh species and is under the constant surveillance of the Isle of Wight Natural History Society.

The woodlands and copses offer other habitats to the island's bird life and blackcap, garden warbler, chiff-chaff and willow warbler may be seen in summer. Species common to the wooded Undercliff include the wren, bluetit, blackbird, robin, great tit, wood-pigeon, jay and the occasional woodpecker.

The Isle of Wight has a large number of long distance walking and nature trails which utilise over 80 miles (128km) of foot and bridle-paths and short sections of modern roads. They pass through woodlands, farmlands and downland country and link up with the 65 mile (104km) Isle of Wight Coastal Path. They provide an intimate view of the island and their detailed guide leaflets give botanical and zoological information as well as notes on geological formations and on features of historical significance.

CLIMATE

The Isle of Wight, by British standards, is noted for its warm sunny summers and mild winters, factors which have played major roles in its popularity as a holiday island and place for retirement. In general terms, the climate is transitional between the maritime conditions of the south-west peninsula and the more 'continental' characteristics of south-east England, though its insularity ensures the prevalence of marine influences at all times. The island's mild winters are reflected in the rarity of snowfall and a long growing season. The low average rainfall totals in spring and early summer coincide with long hours of sunshine.

The general character of the island's winter weather is dependent on the relative strength and position of the Azores high pressure system and the frequency, intensity and path of Atlantic cyclonic depressions. These are also the major summer controls, but the high pressure system now lies further north and is of greater strength, ideally bringing more settled conditions. Of equal significance to these broad climatic controls are a number of local factors which in an insular setting produce a variety of microclimates within a comparatively small area. Aspect, exposure or shelter, are chiefly responsible for such differences which are often reflected in changes in vegetation patterns and plant associations. Within the Shanklin area alone, for example, the chine, the cliffs and the downs above, all provide a different type of climate, but it is the Undercliff and the Ventnor region that best illustrates the effects of local climate. The protection afforded by the downlands from northerly winds, and the southern aspect, means that this part of the island escapes many of the vagaries of the English winter. This was the sole reason for Ventnor's Victorian reputation as a health resort and today, like Sandown and Shanklin, its popularity is still related to its sunshine record.

3 PREHISTORIC AND ROMAN WIGHT

Even in 1880, at the time this villa was discovered,
the owner of this very property in his home on the
other side of the Down, was still suffering the discomforts
of an inadequately heated dining-room which his
Roman predecessor, 17 hundred years before him, would
not have tolerated for an instant.

Cecil Aspinall-Oglander

THOUGH archaeological evidence is particularly sparse for its earliest cultural phases, a combination of favourable environmental factors ensured the Isle of Wight an almost unbroken succession of prehistoric cultures from Stone Age times onwards. During the geological Pleistocene, which coincided with the Palaeolithic or Old Stone Age (*c*500,000–*c*10,000 BC), much of England north of the Thames and Severn estuaries was periodically ice-bound with regions to the south experiencing tundra conditions. Not surprisingly, such periods supported little or no life and the arrival of primitive man in southern England is related to phases of climatic amelioration. Initially, these occurred as warmer interglacials separating the main onslaughts or Arctic ice and they made practicable the migration of small bands of Lower Stone Age hunters into southern England, which was then physically co-extensive with the continent.

Evidence of intermittent settlement comes from a number of open gravel sites in what was to become southern Hampshire and the Isle of Wight. These often occur between 80 and 100ft

Literary legacies: *(above)* Farringford, the home of the poet Tennyson – now a hotel *(British Tourist Authority)*; *(below left)* the tree presented to Tennyson by the Duchess of Sutherland and planted by the Italian liberator Garibaldi in 1864 *(British Tourist Authority)*; *(below right)* on a visit to Shanklin, Longfellow was moved to write these six sentimental lines on a fountain amongst its old thatched cottages *(British Tourist Authority)*

FARRINGFORD
"THE HOME OF TENNYSON"

THE
GARIBALDI TREE

THIS TREE WAS GIVEN
TO TENNYSON BY THE
DUCHESS OF SUTHERLAND
AND WAS PLANTED BY
GARIBALDI THE ITALIAN
LIBERATOR WHEN HE
VISITED THE POET IN
APRIL 1864

O Traveller, stay thy weary feet;
Drink of this fountain pure and sweet;
It flows for rich and poor the same.
Then go thy way, remembering still
The wayside well beneath the hill,
The cup of water in His name.
Longfellow

(*above*) Another literary legacy: Swinburne spent his childhood in the parish of Bonchurch where he now lies buried in the nineteenth-century churchyard (*British Tourist Authority*); (*left*) the oldest house in Brading and probably in the island. It is now incongruously the home of a wax museum

(27–33m) above sea level and the early flint hand axes and associated implements belong to what archaeologists term the Acheulian cultural phase. A number of sites, including some in the Isle of Wight, are associated with faunal remains such as the teeth of *Elephas primigenius*. A small diorama at Carisbrooke Castle Museum depicts such a hairy mammoth standing proudly, yet forlornly (as if extinction was expected), amidst scanty vegetation of coarse grass and stunted birch trees.

The birch was a herald of the long and irregular process of climatic improvement which followed the final retreat of the ice. Such woods, followed by pine and, later, mixed oak forests with thick undergrowths, reflect this amelioration which, accompanied by corresponding changes in fauna, enabled Mesolithic or Middle Stone Age man (*c*7000–*c*3200 BC) to lead an itinerant existence hunting or snaring in woodlands and fishing in the rivers, lakes and marshes that abounded in the aftermath of the ice. The physical separation of Britain from the continent (and probably the Isle of Wight from the mainland) took place in early Mesolithic times, but for most of the period it was still possible, at least at low tides, to move freely over The Solent area and it is doubtful whether the English Channel and North Sea provided major barriers to movement.

River gravels, beaches and lightly forested sandy heaths were the favoured sites of the Mesolithic hunters and fishers. Their microlithic flint implements used, when hafted into wood, for arrowpoints, fish-spears, scrapers, saws and axes, have been found in a number of localities in the Isle of Wight, particularly along the Medina estuary, at Brighstone and Sandown Bays and at Freshwater where the latter sites are related to the former extension of the West Yar River. Mesolithic remains have also been found around Newtown and Bembridge Harbours. All of these sites represent temporary encampments and their location on low ground near the coast, an estuary or a wooded valley, reflect the significant economic factors of hunting and fishing.

37

FARMERS AND METALLURGISTS

The arrival in Britain of small groups of mixed farmers from the continent heralded the beginning of the Neolithic or New Stone Age (*c*3200–*c*1850 BC). It marked the transition from an essentially parasitical economy to one where some control of food supply was possible. In terms of the archaeological record the Neolithic is marked by the occurrence of polished stone axes, pottery, the bones of domesticated animals, and evidence of cultivation and trade. The lighter soils of the Chalk uplands and ridges were particularly suited to primitive cultivation which, initially, was of the shifting type using hand implements or a rudimentary plough. This, together with the increasing numbers of domesticated animals (sheep, goats and cattle) and the drier, warmer, climate that characterised the British Neolithic, led to a substantial reduction of natural vegetation, particularly on woodland margins. Few habitation sites are known, but these farmer-pastoralists left important monuments in their long barrows which were essentially communal burial mounds. These have survived on Afton, Arreton and Niton Downs though it is often difficult to determine whether they belong to the Neolithic or to subsequent peoples.

The transition from the Neolithic to the Bronze Age (*c*1850–*c*550 BC) came with the immigration of central European peoples who brought with them a new technology which included the knowledge and use of copper, bronze and gold. Numerous round barrows on the island's downlands point to a considerable population during the Bronze Age, though unlike the Neolithic peoples they buried their dead in single graves. Excavations at South Arreton, Brading, Brighstone, Calbourne and Afton Down have revealed battle-axes, wristguards, tanged arrow-heads and daggers. Many consider that the best and most varied of the Bronze Age barrows are the eight on Brook Down, Brighstone, though all have robbers' hollows at their centres and little is known of their contents.

The last major Bronze Age movement of peoples into southern Britain took place around 1200 BC. Their important innovation was a settled agriculture based on some established form of land tenure, crop rotation and the use of the traction plough. Animals were penned in winter in embanked enclosures and this undoubtedly aided the collection of dung for use on the adjacent fields. The so-called 'Celtic fields', consisting of groups of small embanked parcels of land 0·5–1·5 acres in area, may date from this period. Remnants occur on the island's southward-facing downland slopes near Calbourne, Chillerton, Brading and Rowborough. This Bronze Age farming system set an economic pattern which remained virtually unchanged until the Roman conquest.

The Iron Age
The British Iron Age has no obvious beginning for it evolved steadily through the Middle and Late Bronze Ages, though in physical terms it was marked by a change to a cooler and wetter climate. Early iron objects were rare possessions, but the ultimate commonplace use of the metal proved to be an influential force on the landscape in terms of forest and other clearances. One of the hallmarks of the Iron Age was the hill-top fort which was largely a reflection of growing land hunger and increasingly unsettled conditions. On Chillerton Down the single rampart and ditch earthwork, though unfinished and subsequently disturbed, is a typical Iron Age upland fort whose defences enclose an area of about ten hectares. In view of the fact that this is the only Iron Age defensive structure so far identified on the island it may be regarded as the local tribal capital around which a population lived in small farming communities. The existence of just one defensive structure may reflect the protection the Isle of Wight obtained from its insularity, for open hostilities and local skirmishes were certainly common amongst the tribes of the mainland.

Three groups of Iron Age Celts, known to archaeologists as A, B and C (though not necessarily in chronological sequence), have been identified in southern Britain. Ptolemy's map of

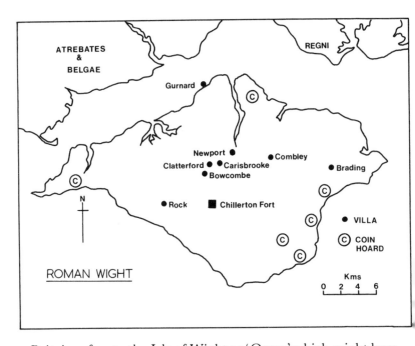

ATREBATES & BELGAE

REGNI

Gurnard

© C

Newport
Clatterford ● ●Carisbrooke
●Bowcombe

●Combley

●Brading

© C

N

●Rock ■ Chillerton Fort

© C

© C ●VILLA

© C COIN HOARD

© C

© C

ROMAN WIGHT

Kms
0 2 4 6

Britain refers to the Isle of Wight as 'Occes' which might have been the title of an independent tribe. Archaeological evidence tends to suggest, however, that prior to the Roman conquest, the island was tributary to the Iron Age C tribal area of the Atrebates, a Belgic people who, with the Catuvellauni, were amongst the most powerful and warlike in Britain. The Belgae, who had previously fled the Low Countries to escape the Roman armies, established settlements or trading posts on the island's main rivers and the earliest evidence of their presence comes from Mount Joy, a chalk hill-top a little to the south-west of Newport. In 1915, grave-diggers working in a public cemetery discovered wares which included Belgae saucepan pots and bead-rimmed vessels. The most important find, however, was a fragment of a Roman wine amphora of a type known to have been imported before the Roman invasion, and occasionally found in the graves of Belgae chieftains. Brading, Knighton and the Medina estuary at Newport also provide evidence of continued Belgae activity.

Ictis

Largely on account of its Roman name, Vectis, there have been a number of attempts to link the island with Ictis, the British tin-exporting island mentioned by the Sicilian writer Diodorus Siculus. Around 25 BC he recorded that Cornish tin, en route through France to Mediterranean and other destinations, was carried 'to a certain island off Britain called Ictis (Icta). During the ebb of the tide the intervening space is left dry'. Most authorities hold that this reference is to St Michael's Mount, near Penzance, though in 1905 Clement Reid maintained that the island in question was Wight, for in Diodorus' time St Michael's Mount would have been nothing more than a mound in a swamp. Arguing on mainly geological grounds with little archaeological support, Reid claimed that Vectis was linked to the mainland by a causeway between the Pennington Marshes in Hampshire and a point near Yarmouth where the Bembridge limestone reaches the coast.

Both the Phoenicians and Greeks brought tin from Cornwall and the latter, to cut out their competitors, opened up a land route through Marseilles which might have led along the English coast to the Isle of Wight, as being the most direct line to Cornwall. Thus more plausible theories suggest that the ford or causeway in question extended from Lepe on the mainland to Gurnard Bay and tradition has it that an ancient British road linked Lepe with Cornwall. Certainly there are interesting place-names along it, such as Stansa Bay and Stans Ore Point, derived from the Latin *stannum*, meaning tin. From Gurnard, once the site of a Roman villa, the island section of this route might have led due south to Puckaster Bay near Niton which claims to be a port in ancient times. Place-names again offer some guide to the direction of this route. Between Gurnard and Newport there was once a straight road called Rue Street though today, because of Parkhurst Forest, only sections of it remain, but straggling its northern part is the modern settlement of Rew Street. Off this road was Gonneville Lane represented by modern Gunville to the north-east of Newport. It is interesting that Rue and Gonneville are place-names on the Somme which might have been the receiving point for the tin. The road continued south through Chillerton Street and Chale Street to the Niton area where place-names are again suggestive. Puckaster, apparently, is derived from Latin and a nearby farm, now a famous inn, was called Buddle, this being a large wooden frame used to wash metalliferous ores.

Such theories, of course, are neither a hundred per cent convincing nor fanciful. Many argue that though the coast at Niton offers a short crossing to northern France the business-like tin merchants would not have found the land movement of ores to the island practicable. They would have been shipped from Cornwall directly, making use of transpeninsular crossings in Brittany and then the Garonne valley to the Mediterranean. If, however, the Phoenicians and Greeks found the island inconvenient for their activities, there were others, because of its position, climate and indeed its oysters, who regarded it as an attractive and acceptable location.

VECTIS

The island's first contact with the Romans came in AD 43, or early in AD 44, at the time when the Second Legion, under the command of Vespasian, was occupied in mounting the offensive against the west of England. It is unfortunate that no first-hand account of these operations exists, but Suetonius' *Lives of the Caesars* records that Vespasian fought thirty battles in Britain, reduced two powerful tribes (probably the Durotriges of the Dorset area and the Atrebates and Belgae of Hampshire) and conquered over twenty native fortresses. No names are given, except that of the Isle of Wight (Vectis), which was reduced to unconditional surrender. The inference, therefore, is that the island was taken by force, but unlike the mainland there is no evidence of early Roman fortification and, as yet, little record of military action. The island's only fort at Carisbrooke appears to have been built at a much later period as part of the general Roman defences against

Germanic incursions. It was rectangular in form, some 440 by 480ft (134 × 146m) with walls over 10ft (3m) thick, traces of which can be identified in the Norman masonry of Carisbrooke Castle. Following its conquest, Vectis, for the purposes of Roman provincial administration, was included with the tribal area or *civitas* of the Belgae, an artificial creation which covered most of Hampshire, central Wiltshire, the northern half of Somerset and a small part of Gloucestershire.

In a province infamous for its cold and damp weather the comparatively equable climate of the Isle of Wight must have proved an attraction to the Romans. Unlike the mainland there is, as yet, no evidence that they built roads and towns, but the Romans quarried and exported the limestones of Binstead, Quarr and Bembridge and appear to have turned Vectis into a prosperous farming area based on peasant holdings and Romano-British villa estates. Eight villas have so far been recognised, but it is debatable whether they were inhabited by retired or wealthy Roman army officers. British villas mostly represent the adoption of Roman standards, in greater or lesser degree, by natives of substance.

With the exception of the villa at Gurnard (discovered in 1864, but subsequently destroyed by coastal erosion), the remaining seven are closely associated with the island's central range of chalk downs, a distribution which suggests a broad similarity in villa farming practice. Animal bones at Newport, Rock and Brading attest to the importance of sheep-farming and cattle-raising and the presence of stone rotary querns for hand-grinding corn emphasises the significance of cultivation. Wheat, barley and oats were the main crops but rye, peas and beans were also grown and the discovery of cherry stones at Brading might indicate some form of fruit farming, though the extent of this activity, as indeed viticulture, can only be surmised.

The Brading villa
Early Romano-British villas were simple and unpretentious yet with time, provided they were economically viable

enterprises, comforts and luxuries were added. The description of the villa near Brading as 'a miniature Pompeii' is Wight magniloquence, yet nonetheless, it is the finest on the island and its famous mosaic pavements have rendered it one of the most visited in Britain. The villa was discovered by chance in 1879 and excavations, which began a year later, revealed an estate of some considerable importance. It was built towards the end of the second century AD and, judging from its coins, was occupied for about 200 years before abandonment.

A winged corridor house occupying the western side of a courtyard some 180ft square (55m square) is the basis of its plan, with ranges of farm buildings enclosing the northern and southern sides. The courtyard is open to the east where the land slopes down to the coast, which, in Roman times, would have been closer to the front of the villa. Such an arrangement appears to have evolved to take full advantage of the natural attractions of the site as well as to meet the growing farming needs of the estate. To the north of the villa on Brading Down is a fine example of an ancient field system with small rectangular plots. Though it is not known whether they were worked from the farm, their steep lynchets, rising as much as 3m, suggest that they were cultivated over a long period and were probably contemporary with the villa for part of the time.

The owners of the villa, at least in its later stages, must have been persons of importance. The living quarters, consisting of some twelve rooms, were arranged around a hall or corridor and the central range of rooms were probably lit by clerestory windows, for an abundance of glass is associated with the site. In six of these rooms are the remains of a series of what were expensive mosaic floors or pavements, reputed to be some of the finest in Britain. Villa owners appreciated classical and mythological themes and the decorated scenes at Brading include Medusa with snakes, Orpheus and lyre, Perseus holding the gorgon's head, tritons, nereids and pictorial representations of the elements. Though only five of the original nine panels survive, a mosaic pavement in the entrance hall is without parallel in the Roman Empire. The bust of Bacchus occupies the central roundel around which are a series of evocative allegorical scenes whose meaning is still subject to question. The walls of the hall were also richly decorated with painted plaster, the remnants of which depict a parrot-like bird and a still life design of a green basket with purple plums. The west wing also contained the bathroom suite and a number of rooms had hypocaust heating which involved the drawing in of hot air from a wood-fired furnace outside the building. It circulated beneath the floors which were supported on pillars of rectangular tiles and use was also made of the rising heat by constructing special ducts or flues in the walls which made use of rectangular clay tubes known as box-flue tiles.

The range of rooms on the north side of the courtyard clearly underwent many changes of plan and use. The complete building was more than 135ft (45m) long by 50ft (17m) wide and might initially have been built as a long aisled barn shared by livestock, produce and farm equipment. Subsequently, its western end was partitioned into a commodious suite of rooms again with hypocaust heating and probably occupied by the farmer-bailiff in charge of the estate. The eastern part continued its role as a barn or workshop. The southern side of the courtyard was occupied by another large building (150ft (49m) by 33ft (10m)) whose western end may have been the quarters for farm workers. Nothing is known about the social organisation of the Brading estate but where there was a resident staff of workers, either slaves or crofter-labourers, their accommodation nearly always takes the form of a barn-dwelling ranged on one side of the courtyard. Between the living quarters and the northern block a semi-circular ornamental fountain or *nymphaeum* probably had a quasi-religious function.

Various artefacts provide a fairly detailed view of the material culture of the Brading villa which appears to have reached its maximum development in the fourth century. At all times, however, Brading was a profit-making estate and pleasureable luxuries, such as its mosaics, could only be obtained through a substantial farming income. The villa's complete agricultural orientation is epitomised in its corn-drying oven which was a necessity in a damp climate. It came to be housed in the entrance hall of the main building-block and, cut into the mosaic floor, it worked on a similar principle to the hypocaust system. Wood and charcoal were used in the Brading furnaces, but discoveries of coal and anthracite from south-west Wales suggest a certain amount of trade in fuels.

The Newport villa

Though Brading is the island's best preserved villa, the one at Newport (off Avondale Road) is not without considerable interest. It was discovered in 1926 and excavated shortly afterwards. The original site was a south-east facing slope leading down to the Medina and, dating from the second century, the villa represents the final stage in an occupation which began with Iron Age settlement. Like others of its type the Newport villa is a winged corridor house which faced on to a central courtyard. Its outbuildings, however, have not really been located, so the dimensions of the courtyard are uncertain. The corridor (perhaps verandah) provided access to the seven rooms of the central range and to the wings. The house was smaller than that of Brading and its geometrically designed mosaics, only fragments of which survive, are inferior.

One of the main features of the Newport villa is its complex bathroom suite attached to the west wing. It comprises an apodyterium or changing room, three water apartments inscribed according to their temperatures (frigidarium, tepidarium and caldarium) and a sudatorium for massage and manicure. Enough has survived to show clearly the workings of this bath suite which was heated by a main hypocaust furnace on the same principles as Brading. A small hypocaust system was also provided for a single room in the east wing.

A bathhouse in a Roman villa, no matter how simple, was evidence of advancing civilisation. At Newport, however, one indication of the villa's decline in circumstances (probably as a result of Saxon raids in the second half of the third century) is the subsequent sealing up of the hypocaust system and the use of the baths as stores. It is tempting to equate the tiled fireplace to this period for this was a rare feature in a Roman house. It is unusually elaborate, having tiled wings enclosing it on either side, and the remains of a tiled corbel and possibly a plaster hood, blackened with smoke, were discovered in the vicinity.

Other Roman sites

The villas at Brading and Newport are the only ones which have been systematically and scientifically studied. The Victorian excavators of Rock and Clatterford appear to have provided no plans of these villas and the work at Carisbrooke by W. Spickernell after 1859 also left much to be desired. Here, however, early drawings show low walls with painted designs and at least one mosaic pavement whose motif was a central vase of flowers surrounded by a geometrical border. The Carisbrooke villa is now incorporated into the vicarage garden and is largely hidden beneath grass and shrubs. Further excavations at Bowcombe, Combley and within the Newport district will, hopefully, provide fresh information on the character and development of the Vectis villas.

To date no villas have been discovered on the Chalk and Greensand areas of South Wight though a series of coin hoards discovered at Wroxall, Hyde, Ventnor, Sandown, Limerstone and Farringford (as well as two hoards in the north) suggests that this was by no means an unprosperous area in Roman times. Roman and Belgic pottery attest to the occupation of Ventnor and the Undercliff and it seems likely that this part of the island was occupied by the less durable, in terms of archaeological survival, native settlements. An earthwork and hut foundation excavated on Limestone Down near Shorwell in 1932 is one of the few sites of this type so far identified. The relationship between native settlements and the villas remains an archaeological problem.

As suggested in the archaeological record of the Newport villa, the growing danger from Saxon pirates left its mark on the Isle of Wight. Their raids were at their height towards the end of the third century, one reason why the inhabitants buried their savings and some did not survive to reclaim them. Between 287 and 293 Carausius, who had elected himself emperor of Britain, began the series of coastal defences known as the 'Saxon Shore'. These forts ran from Norfolk to the Isle of Wight (with others elsewhere in Britain) and held mixed garrisons of soldiers and sailors for intercepting raiders both by land and sea. Carausius was assassinated by his chief finance minister, Allectus, who himself was defeated in 296 by imperial troops off the Isle of Wight. Military and administrative reorganisation followed the return of central government but Vectis fails to feature in these annals.

4 SAXONS AND NORMANS

*then Caedwalla . . . took the Isle of Wight . . . which until that
time had been wholly given up to the worshipping of idols.*

The Venerable Bede, *Opera Historica*

AS elsewhere in southern Britain confusion descends
after the departure of the Romans and the early part of
the so-called Anglo-Saxon period is one of dubious and
insubstantial historical evidence. Not only are documentary
sources contradictory, these, too, are also at variance with
archaeological and place-name evidence which makes the
precise course of settlement difficult to disentangle. The result
has been an astonishing amount of speculation producing
several distinct viewpoints, not to say, academic disputes. 'We
have to grope', as one writer puts it, 'among the tangled
undergrowth of Dark Age history with little more than the
flickering torches of the Chronicles to guide us.'

The written history of the Isle of Wight begins with Bede
who, after relating its Roman occupation, speaks of the Jutish
colonisation of the island and of the lands opposite it on the
mainland. The people of Southern Hampshire he calls *Jutarum
natio*, the Jutish nation, though by the time of his writing this
was part of the West-Saxon kingdom. The Jutes in southern
England present an historical problem and many scholars
favour the view that Bede's reference to them has been over-
interpreted. Yet grave finds on the Isle of Wight and near
Droxford, which include utensils and brooches, are similar in
character to those of Kent which archaeologists have labelled

49

Jutish.One established view is that the early settlers in Wight and southern Hampshire were organised under Jutish leaders who received reinforcements from the continent. The Jutes differed considerably from the Saxons and it has been suggested that Jutish overlords came to Britain not directly from Jutland, but after a settlement period in the Middle Rhinelands. Though the New Forest has not yielded any Jutish objects, it is significant that as late as 1100 the area was referred to as *Ytene* ('of the Jutes') by the local inhabitants.

THE SAXONS

That the *Anglo-Saxon Chronicle* makes no reference to the Jutes is not really surprising for basically it is the story of Alfred the Great's ancestors and, compiled during his reign, it traces or prefabricates the 'Saxon' origin of the House of Wessex. The *Chronicle* is a year by year record, in a number of vernacular annalistic accounts, of the major events in Anglo-Saxon England, but much of it is chronologically unreliable and historians regard its early entries as a confused rendering of mythical events. All seven surviving manuscripts begin with a history of Britain from the invasion by Julius Caesar, and down to the year 891 are based on one account. Thereafter, differing annals were written in different places.

The *Chronicle* begins its story of the rise of Wessex by virtually apotheosising a small band of adventurers led by Cerdic who landed on the Hampshire coast at 'Cerdices ora' in AD 495. In 530, along with Cynric, this semi-legendary, perhaps mythical, chieftain invaded the Isle of Wight as part of the Saxon conquest and consolidation of southern England. The various documentary entries that relate his activities in Hampshire and Wight are contradictory but a decisive battle at Carisbrooke is recorded where the islanders proved no match for the Saxons. Though the *Chronicle* reports that only a few men were slain the outcome was the island's incorporation into the Kingdom of Wessex and it was divided amongst Cerdic's faithful warriors.

Following Cerdic's death Wight was given to (perhaps

reconquered by) his nephew Wihtgar and an associate (or another nephew) known as Stuf! There is one opinion that the island derives its name from Wihtgar who was buried at Carisbrooke, renamed 'Wiht-gara-burh (Wihtgaresburg)' or 'the place where Wihtgar lies'. As plausible as this may sound the Saxon chronicle writers were great inventors and many of their place-name derivations appear a little more than obvious. For instance, the *Chronicle* states that a man called Port, accompanied by his two sons, landed in 501 at a place which came to be known as Portsmouth; the coincidence of names is, of course, startling. As far as the name Wight is concerned it is safer to agree that it derives from the Celtic Ynys-y-Wyth which became more easily the Saxon Weet or Wight.

For the hundred years following the recorded death of Wihtgar, little is known about the Isle of Wight. England, however, was divided into several kingdoms, although there were long periods when those south of the Humber were united under an overlord known, according to a ninth-century authority, as a *Bretwalda*, 'ruler of Britain'. In the latter half of the seventh century Wulfhere of Mercia extended such control over southern England and in 681, probably for political reasons, he ceded Wight and a stretch of the Hampshire coast to Aldewach (Athelwach), ruler of the South Saxons of Sussex and obviously his vassal king. Bede mentions the ceding of two provinces, namely Wight and the land of Meonwaras (the Hampshire coast area) which suggests that the island remained independent of Wessex at this time. Around 686 Caedwalla of Wessex slew Aldewach, conquered the Isle of Wight and settled it with his followers. If the island had indeed been a Jutish colony, from this date, it became an intrinsic part of the West Saxon kingdom.

Wight, according to Bede, was one of the last corners of Britain to receive Christianity, but the method and process of its conversion is enveloped in duplicate and contradictory accounts. Wulfhere, it appears, had endowed a number of religious houses on the mainland and was angered by the scenes and reports of idolatry on the island. His 'converts' were forcibly baptised at Brading. The other story is that Caedwalla, following some sort of local massacre, gave a fourth part of the island, with its inhabitants, to Bishop Wilfrid, for treatment as he saw fit. One-time Bishop of York, Wilfrid was expelled from his diocese for appealing to Rome and subsequently founded a diocese at Selsey. His portion of the island was given to Berwin, one of his clerks, and a priest by the name of Hiddila was appointed to administer the new faith. Brading again appears in this account and it seems likely that it was the site of the island's first church. Though the present building is of Transitional-Norman architecture and much restored, it is traditionally said to have been founded by Wilfrid during the closing years of the seventh century. Thus, in the opinion of many, the church at Brading is the most interesting in the island.

Alfred and the Danes

Under Alfred, whose mother apparently came from the Isle of Wight, Wessex developed as a powerful English kingdom. Internally threatened by Mercia and externally by Scandinavia in the form of the Danes, Alfred developed an elaborate defence plan which centred around the establishment of a large number of fortified *burhs* theoretically capable of resisting the Danish advance. Whether the Isle of Wight was initially safe from attack, or not worth defending, is debatable, but the *Burghal Hidage*, a tenth-century list of the Wessex strongholds, makes no mention of *burhs* on the island. Certainly Wight seems to have fared better than the mainland, yet it has the distinction of the first, albeit unsuccessful, Danish attack in 787. In 896, six years before Alfred's death, there was another attack when six shiploads of Danes landed near Brading. After a fierce battle Alfred's galleys cut off their retreat and the Danes ran aground on the mainland and were executed at Winchester.

During the reign of Alfred and his successors the Danes and other Scandinavians, who had settled in the north and east of England, were gradually brought under the control of the

52

(*above*) Victorian artists such as George Brannon romanticised the scenery of the Isle of Wight. This engraving (1840) is of Freshwater Bay, with the cliffs of Tennyson Down and some exaggerated hills in the distance; (*below*) the famous Buddle Inn at Niton which has smuggling associations

Contrasting cliffs: *(right)* the deeply eroded coloured beds at Alum Bay; *(below)* the chalk cliffs and thinly vegetated downs east of the Needles

English crown. Alfred's son, Edward, effectively governed all of England south of the Humber and managed to maintain the peace for many years. Subsequent rulers, however, were less successful and between 978 and 1016 the annals reflect the foolish policy of Ethelred the Unready in trying to buy off the Danes who took his bribes but persisted in their raiding. Up to the time of the Norman Conquest the Isle of Wight, like much of southern England, was subjected to attacks by Scandinavian marauders who destroyed villages, and either massacred the inhabitants or carried them into slavery. To an England subjected to such pillage the Norman Conquest with its subsequent firm rule and apparent security must have appeared as a blessing.

THE NORMANS

Following William of Normandy's conquest of England, the Isle of Wight retained its separate identity and was not properly incorporated into the English realm until the reign of Edward I (1272–1307). In characteristic Norman fashion William awarded lands and estates to his friends and followers, especially those that had displayed courage and patriotism at the Battle of Hastings. The Isle of Wight was given to William Fitz Osborn, the first of the long line of political and military leaders to whom the Crown has given authority in the island. Fitz Osborn, a kinsman and close friend of the Conqueror, was co-planner of the invasion of England and also acted as Regent for William during his absences in Normandy. On the island he ruled from Carisbrooke Castle where he commissioned the construction of the initial fortified keep and baileys. Like the majority of early Norman castles Carisbrooke contained no masonry buildings but was defended by earthworks and palisades. Ruling the island 'as freely as the King himself held the realm of England', Fitz Osborn promptly deprived the local Saxon landowners of their estates and shared them among his favourites. These included Fitz-Azor, Fitz-Stur and one Hugh de Oglandres whose descendants, after some 900 years, still live on the island at Nunwell House near Brading.

55

T024663

The Domesday Survey

A fairly detailed picture of the landscape and economy of Fitz Osborn's lordship can be gleaned from the *Domesday Book*, the great national survey of William I's newly-conquered lands. Compiled in 1086, on a tenurial basis, its primary object was to provide information for the purposes of royal taxation. It thus records the amount of land held by the lord of the manor, the number of serfs, villeins and others who formed his tenantry, the number of ploughs they possessed, the amount of woodland, meadow, pasture and other resources, and also the former and present value of the manor. The interpretation of these entries is often problematic, but the Isle of Wight, together with the New Forest, is fortunate in having a separate section devoted to it with its own schedule of land-holders.

In 1086 the island's total population is recorded as 1068 and around 88 place-names are mentioned. A characteristic feature of the island was the sparsity of village and other settlement on much of the ill-drained clays and patches of infertile gravels of the north. Waterlogged and acid soils were obviously not as attractive to medieval farmers as the varied lands of the centre and south where villages were frequent. The average *Domesday* population densities give ten to the square mile for the south and three for the north and this distinction is also reflected in the numbers and densities of plough-teams.

Woodland was a vital resource to the medieval rural economy and apart from a few miscellaneous references it is recorded in the Isle of Wight in terms of pannage (carrying capacity) for swine. It is doubtful whether the woodland entries are a complete record for little is recorded for the northern clay areas where (as now) woodlands would have flourished. Again, only small amounts of pasture and meadowland are mentioned and it appears that the island possessed only three salt pans and one fishery. The location of the latter was either at Perreton (between Merstone and Arreton) on the east Yar or at Preston in St Helens at the mouth of the same river.

Compared to many areas of southern and eastern England, *Domesday* hardly presents a prosperous picture of the Isle of

Wight though some if its resources, particularly its forest land, gave it some note of distinction. Parkhurst, today one of the island's largest areas of woodland, is not specifically mentioned in the survey but there is reference to 'the Park of the King' at nearby Watchingwell, and there is no doubt that Parkhurst was an ancient woodland several times its present size, probably stretching from the Medina to the Newtown estuary.

In medieval parlance the term 'forest' was used in a legal sense to denote royal hunting rights and was far from synonymous with woodland, though all 'forested' areas contained a nucleus of wood—sometimes large tracts of wooded territory. The character of Parkhurst before the Norman Conquest is obscure, but it seems certain that after 1066 the 'forest law' and 'forest courts' of Normandy were introduced into England on a large scale. This severe code of law was enforced to secure the preservation of certain wild animal species, especially deer, and in later centuries there are references to Parkhurst as a royal chase where the visiting monarch and the island lords went hunting. Until the fourteenth century the forest seems to have followed the same line of descent as Carisbrooke Castle.

Domesday also mentions the Priory of Carisbrooke which was founded by Fitz Osborn. It was a cell of the Benedictine Abbey of Lyre in Normandy to which it sent dues from its lands and possessions in the island. The Priory, dedicated to the Blessed Virgin, held six churches, two of which are recorded in the entries for Bowcombe and Arreton manors, but no information is given on the others. Subsequent grants were given to Carisbrooke Priory and Henry III's confirmation charter to Lyre Abbey particularises its possessions throughout the Isle of Wight. By this time it held the churches of Carisbrooke, Arreton, Freshwater, Godshill, Whippingham, Newtown and Newchurch.

William Fitz Osborn never saw the survey which detailed his lordship for he was killed in battle at Ravenchoven, near Cassel, in 1071. The island passed to his son, Roger de Breteuil, who held the island until 1078 when his rebellion against King William led to life imprisonment. Wight then seems to have been given to Odo, Bishop of Bayeux and Earl of Kent. He was William's half-brother and though patriotic in commissioning the famous tapestry, he proved to be another rebel by organising an expedition to Rome to overthrow the Church. William intercepted his fleet in the Channel where he was arrested, not in his ecclesiastical capacity but as Earl of Kent, and brought to Carisbrooke. He was then taken to Rouen and imprisoned.

The de Redvers family

William the Conqueror died at Rouen in 1087 and it seems that William II took possession of the island until his death in the New Forest in 1100. Family and dynastic troubles followed but under Henry I (1100–1135) came the first grant of the lordship to the de Redvers family, a powerful baronial house who kept the island, almost on terms of independent sovereignty, for nearly two hundred years. Originally from Reviers in Normandy, they were Lords of Vernon and Nehou and were allied to the royal house by marriage. Richard de Redvers stood high in Henry I's favour and his son, Baldwin, who inherited the lordship (1107–1155) consolidated what his father had gained, for with great holdings in Devon and elsewhere, including the hundred of Christchurch, the de Redvers had about as large and compact a unit of territory as any Norman lord was permitted to hold.

Baldwin de Redvers, who also bore the title Earl of Devon, replaced the Norman stockaded fort at Carisbrooke with 'a stately castle built of hewn stone'. Though originally higher, this shell keep, an irregular polygon in plan, still survives, and a long and steep flight of steps leads up the great artificial mound on which it stands. One of the baileys was also enclosed with a curtain wall much of which again still stands. Baldwin is also credited with the founding of Quarr Abbey in 1132. Built of local stone from the nearby quarries which probably gave it its name, a site was chosen close to the coast, about a quarter of a mile east of Wootton Creek. The abbey, consecrated on 1 June

1150, was originally tenanted by monks from the Normandy monastery of Savigny and like most medieval religious foundations it prospered by careful management and successive endowments. Later writings talk of its 'great market kept three days in every week at the crossway some twelve score yards from the house to the south-west'. In 1130 special licence was obtained to fortify the place against sea attacks and the remaining stone wall, with its sea gate, can still be traced. Quarr naturally suffered the fate of most religious houses during the reign of Henry VIII, and following its dissolution its stone was sold to George Mills, a Southampton merchant. Excavations in 1890 revealed the plan of the abbey whose church architecture and that of the greater part of its conventual buildings was of the mid-thirteenth century. At Quarr, Baldwin, his wife and his son were buried, together with other distinguished personages, including Lady Cicely, second daughter of Edward IV.

On the death of Henry I the royal succession was disputed and Baldwin de Redvers sided with Henry's daughter, the Empress Maud, against Stephen (1135–54), the last of the Norman kings. Following his defeat at Exeter in 1136 Baldwin retreated to Carisbrooke where Stephen forced his surrender. A period of exile followed, but in 1153 he was reinstated in the lordship. For nearly a century and a half Baldwin's descendants held sway on the Isle of Wight, but with one exception they are misty figures who are little more than names in the Obituary of Montebourg—the Normandy abbey of which the de Redvers were patrons.

The exception, and last of this particular line, was Isabel de Fortz (Fortibus), Countess of Devon and Albemarle and Lady of the Isle of Wight from 1262 to 1293. As daughter of Baldwin de Redvers IV and widow of William de Fortz she is one of the most notable owners of Carisbrooke who, it is reported, was one of the wealthiest non-royal ladies in the kingdom. Energetic, beautiful, intelligent and resilient are some of the adjectives used to describe her and she lived in Carisbrooke in pomp and regal splendour. Isabel was responsible for rebuilding the Great Hall, the adjoining chapel of St Peter, the Great Chamber, the 'New' (in 1275) Chamber of the Countess and the wells and well-house.

In 1293, from her death-bed at her manor of Stockwell, Isabel surrendered the lordship and other property to Edward I in return for the payment of 6,000 marks. Having no heirs this transaction was the outcome of many years of indecision and it carries with it a strong suspicion of foul play. The purchase price was ridiculously small and historians will long argue as to whether, or not, Isabel was obliged, cheated or forced to sell.

The Isle of Wight thus became an integral part of the English realm and though titular lords of the island and castle continued to be appointed it was no longer a semi-independent fiefdom. After 1495 the title lord was changed to captain and this continued for nearly a hundred years when the title governor came into use, and this has continued until the present day.

5   CASTLES, CAPTAINS AND GOVERNORS

That Isle which jutting out into the sea so far,
Her offspring traineth up in excercise of war;
Those pirates to put back that oft purloin her trade,
Or Spaniards, or the French attempting to invade.

Michael Drayton, *Polyolbion*, 1622

FROM the thirteenth century onwards the Isle of Wight was very much a bulwark of England. Within a year of its incorporation into the English realm, Edward I (1272–1307) declared war on France, instituting the so-called Hundred Years War which, in fact, lasted for more than a century. Enemy raiders were common in the Channel and there was a constant invasion scare and state of emergency. Watch and ward was necessary on the island which was particularly vulnerable and strategically attractive to the French, especially in view of the ever-increasing naval significance of Portsmouth. All landowners with property valued at £20 and over had to provide an armed horseman for the island's defences and watches and warning beacons were maintained on commanding hills. Every able-bodied man was held liable to serve in case of enemy invasion and various restrictions were placed on the export of grain and cattle.

Edward further demanded the services of the island's knights to fight for him against Scotland which, to complicate continental politics, had declared itself an ally of France. The lords stubbornly refused, arguing that they were not bound to the King's service beyond The Solent. Such rebellious spirits under a feudal system warranted royal reprisals, but there is no record of punishment by the Crown. This independence, however, almost certainly motivated Edward II's (1307–27) attempt to foist his favourite, Piers Gaveston, as absolute lord of the islanders by granting him the Castle and Honour of Carisbrooke, but not the Lordship of the Island. The baronage refused to accept him and Gaveston was obliged to relinquish his titles in favour of Edward's new-born son, Edward, Earl of Chester.

THE FRENCH ATTACKS

Wight was subjected to French attacks on a number of occasions during the fourteenth century and the absence of coastal defences often made it an easy target, especially when help was cut off from the mainland. Edward III (1327–77) kept tight control over the island for it was no longer prudent, as in Norman times, to trust it to the keeping of a near-independent magnate. Political tensions between England and France reached a climax in 1340 with Edward's claim to the French throne and defence of the south coast, particularly the Isle of Wight, was a major imperative. The local lords, again called upon to provide men-at-arms, were forbidden to leave the island; those that did were deemed rebellious and forfeited their estates and properties. In an attempt to strengthen earlier defences, Wight was divided into regions each with a local militia of 100 to 200 men under the control of a commander, usually the landlord, who was aided by a lieutenant. Warning beacons and pillion-riders to spread the alarm formed part of this defence system which was elaborate for its time.

In 1355, Edward granted the Castle, Lordship and Honour of Carisbrooke to his eldest daughter Isabel, Dame de Coucy, Duchess of Bedford. She had married a French nobleman, a hostage at her father's court, and they both enjoyed the revenues of the island until the accession of Richard II (1377–99) when de Coucy chose to resign his English honours and returned to France. 1377 also witnessed the most serious of the French raids when, after landing at Yarmouth, they advanced inland, slaughtering and pillaging en route. It is reported that women and children sought refuge in Shalfleet church, whose surviving Norman tower 30ft square, and with walls 5ft thick, was obviously built as a defensive structure. Further inland the islanders took refuge at Carisbrooke which the French were unable to take, suffering heavy losses in an ambush at neighbouring Newport.

The period of Richard's reign was one of mounting French threats. The island was governed by Crown officers until 1385 when Richard granted it to his mother's first husband, William de Montacute, Earl of Salisbury. Though little known to history, many scholars regard de Montacute as a great Englishman whose varied career and credentials were used at all times to serve his country. As a soldier he served at Crécy and Poitiers; as a naval commander he was victorious in the sea battle with the Spanish off Winchelsea in 1370; as a diplomatist and negotiator he represented his country on many missions to the continent. De Montacute died in 1397 and was succeeded by Edward, Earl of Rutland.

In 1402, during the reign of Henry IV (1399–1413), the French returned to the Isle of Wight, but hastened home after burning just two villages. They were back in two years and landed again in 1417 only to be driven out by the local militia. For much of this period the island's defender was Edward of Norwich, Earl of Cambridge, Rutland and Cork, and later Duke of York. He governed from 1397 to 1405 and from 1409 to 1415. The four years when he was in eclipse as far as island affairs were concerned was when he was suspected of being part of a plot against the King, his cousin. For this period, and in exchange for part of her dower, the island went to Queen Joanna of Navarre. York regained the island in 1409 but died in the French campaign of 1415, where he is said to have suffocated in the mêlée under the weight of his armour. His body was returned to England and Philippa, his widow, held the island until her death in 1431.

The French attack of 1417 was the last until the reign of Henry VIII, but cumulatively they had reduced the island to a miserable state, as had pestilence and heavy exactions. Many landowners were forced to leave for the mainland and the island's defences left much to be desired. Carisbrooke, which was still the island's major strongpoint, was described in the mid-fifteenth century as being 'nother stuffed with men and harneys, nother with gonnes, gonnepowder, cross bowes, long bowes, arrowes, long speres, axes and gleyves as such a place suld be in tyme of werre . . .'.

The island's situation largely protected it from the effects of the Wars of the Roses, but in 1488, Sir Edward de Woodville induced some forty island gentlemen and four hundred yeomen to join him in aiding the Duke of Brittany against the King of France. Tradition asserts that from this Battle of St Aubins only one boy returned to tell the tale. The effect of these heavy losses upon an already sparsely populated island can be judged from an Act of Parliament passed the following year. In it the island was described as 'desolate and not inhabited, but occupied with beasts and cattle, so that if hasty remedy be not provided, the Isle cannot long be kept and defended, but open and ready to the hands of the King's enemies, which God forbid.'

TUDOR AND STUART DEFENCES

Wars with France seem to have governed the island's history from Plantagenet to Tudor times. Certainly throughout much of his reign Henry VIII, who had broken with the Pope, was engaged in a troubled rapprochement between his potential enemies, Francis I of France and the Hapsburg or Holy Roman Emperor, Charles V. In 1520 Henry entered into an alliance with Charles, but a reconciliation between the latter and Francis meant that for the rest of his reign Henry would be fighting France and the vulnerability of England's south and east coasts was again felt.

In 1538, Henry embarked on a comprehensive scheme of

coastal defence which entailed the construction of a chain of forts from Deal in Kent to St Mawes and Pendennis in Cornwall. Blockhouses or bulwarks were also proposed for every haven and possible landing place and although many were never built there was a concerted effort to protect the entire coast from Milford Haven to Hull. Henry's contributions to the architecture of Hampshire and the Isle of Wight, therefore, are the mainland castles at Calshot, Hurst, Netley and Southsea and their counterparts on the island at Yarmouth, East and West Cowes, and Sandown, thereby providing each of the important areas of The Solent and Spithead with a defensive strongpoint. The two 'Cow Towers' (hence, probably, the name Cowes), flanking the entrance to the Medina estuary, were the earliest of Henry's defences on the Isle of Wight, though little remains of them today.

As well as the castles the island's defence was entrusted to a local 'home guard' and was divided into ten districts, each providing a *centon* or company of armed men, commanded by an officer called a *centoner*. Each *centon* consisted of between 150 and 200 men, armed with a variety of weapons which included muskets, culverins, bows and arrows and a miscellaneous collection of bills and pikes. A small number of mounted men were also attached to each *centon*.

The French siege of 1545 came as a retaliatory assault, following Henry's capture of Boulogne a year earlier. Admiral D'Annibault with an armada of 150 sailing transports carrying, it is said, 60,000 men, sailed into The Solent when the king and his forces were at Portsmouth. Keeping beyond the reach of coastal and naval guns the French simultaneously landed at three places on the island's eastern coasts, including the Sandown area where an additional fort was under construction. The islanders were ready and those that landed at Seaview were driven back to their boats by archers hidden in the woods of Fairy Hill. Those at Bembridge, after harrying far into the island, were ambushed by the local militia and cut to pieces. Never, since, has an enemy force set foot in the Isle of Wight.

Yarmouth Castle

With the system of defences proving inadequate, Sandown was hastily completed and a new fort was undertaken at Yarmouth, a vulnerable position at the main point of communication between the island's western coast and the mainland. Throughout the Middle Ages, high walls and flanking towers (as at Carisbrooke) offered security against surprise attack and could be successfully defended against assault. The damage they might sustain from catapults or other throwing engines was limited. Even the best planned medieval castle or walled town could be reduced by the combined devices of siegecraft, but often they offered a very protracted resistance.

The Tudor castles conceived in 1538 largely followed earlier patterns, but the rapid development of artillery during the sixteenth century slowly destroyed the value of traditional fortification, as high walls could be demolished by direct bombardment. By 1545, in Italy and the Low Countries, this style of fortification was being superseded by new military engineering which included lower, reinforced walls pierced by gun-ports and platforms and squat towers to mount defending guns. A major innovation was the pointed or 'arrow-head' bastion which allowed complete coverage of the walls by lateral fire and with a minimum of exposure. This system, something of a secret at first, became well known after the publication of a book on the subject by P. Cattanes in 1554. Yarmouth was the only castle commissioned by Henry VIII which followed this style; it was the first in England and the forerunner of many defences, including the extensive fortifications begun at Berwick on Tweed in 1558.

Yarmouth Castle was built as a rectangular gun-emplacement on the 'King's land' outside the jurisdiction of the borough. By September 1547 it was considered serviceable when the sum of £1000 was paid to the builder of works and for the discharge of the troops who had guarded the operations. Its walls, nearly a hundred feet in length, formed a square with a sharply-pointed bastion or 'flanker' at the south-eastern corner. The defences also consisted of earthworks with a 30ft deep moat. The embankment or platform facing The Solent was designed exclusively for heavy armaments and in 1547 the castle contained three cannons and culverins and twelve smaller guns.

Richard Worsley, son of Sir James Worsley of Appuldurcombe, an intimate acquaintance of the King, was the guiding spirit in Yarmouth's and the island's defence. By this time only Captains of the island were appointed, but they were the effective civil and military governors, and some, like the Worsleys, were men well suited to the responsibility of island defence. Richard Worsley is recorded as putting 'the people in warlike array for the increase of haquebusry' (musketry). He introduced firearms for the island's militia and every parish was required to possess a gun (some of which still survive) with a team to man it. Worsley was also a builder of fortifications and as an expert in the new principles of gunnery he was consulted on the defences of Portsmouth in 1558 and, subsequently, on those of the Channel Islands.

The Spanish Threat

During the short reign of Mary (1553–8), Worsley, who was of the reformed faith, was replaced by William Girling, a far less competent Captain, but a Roman Catholic. Worsley returned to public life on Elizabeth I's succession and received the Captaincy again in 1560. The continental threat now came from Spain and his first task was to survey, repair and improve the island's castles and defences. Work began on the strengthening of Carisbrooke, but Worsley died in 1565 with a substantial sum of money owing to him by the Crown for improvements there and at Yarmouth. The 'placeing of the Ordnance' at his own and others' expense was a typical example of Elizabeth's frugal measures.

The real responsibility of preparing the island for the Spanish Armada fell to Sir George Carey (Baron Hunsden) who, as an able soldier and campaigner, adopted the title 'Governor' and lived at Carisbrooke in grand style. He added many domestic buildings but his most important works were the outer lines of defence enclosing the old castle and its baileys. These were constructed between 1597 and 1600 under the direction of Federigo Gianibelli, an Italian engineer of great repute who also had a part in designing the fortifications at Antwerp and Berwick on Tweed. These new defences with angular bastions, four at the corners and the fifth to the west of the main entrance, ensured command with crossfire over the entire ramparts. It was a system which was later elaborated by Marshal Vauban, Louis XIV's engineer, whose refined and complex fortifications were to set new high standards of defensive strength.

For much of this period the Isle of Wight was placed in a state of alert and in May 1588, Carey was informed from London that 'there are reasons to prove that the Spaniards should rather land in the Isle of Wight than in any other place in England'. Three beacons were installed on the commanding Downs in the east, west and south of the island with permanent watches in charge. The approach of less than thirty ships was to be notified by the firing of one beacon; two meant that more than thirty but less than fifty were in sight, and three signified a fleet of more than fifty ships. The island's total home guard strength was 1,856 officers and men which was about one-fifth of the population. Of this number it is recorded that 1,158 were armed with muskets, 109 were archers, 116 were pikemen and 473 had only halberds or bills.

The anticipated perils of the Spanish invasion never came and except for a depletion of its timber reserves for Royal Navy ships, many built at Cowes, the Isle of Wight suffered little from the Spanish threat. In the interim, Carey's post was given to Henry Wriothesley, Earl of Southampton who, as Shakespeare's 'patron', was destined to receive literary as well as political fame. Intrigue, disgrace and banishment punctuated his career at Elizabeth's court, though a death sentence for treason was subsequently commuted to life imprisonment. His freedom and earldom were restored by James I who also renewed his Governorship of the island until his death from fever in 1624 during a campaign in the Low

Countries. Shakespeare's *Venus and Adonis* and *Lucrece* were dedicated to Southampton and opinion identifies him as 'the friend' of the Sonnets. What better memorial (perhaps) can a man have than lines such as

> *For they sweet love remembered such welth brings,*
> *That then I skorne to change my state with Kings.*

Throughout the reigns of James I (1603–25) and Charles I (1625–49) the island's defences received considerable attention. In 1609 Sandown and Yarmouth castles were repaired to the cost of £300. At the latter this included a length of new sea wall to protect the moat, two corner buttresses (one of which bears the date and cipher of James I), and an addition of a top storey to the living accommodation. Yet in 1623, a report by John Burnley indicated that further repairs and alterations were necessary as did subsequent reports in 1625 and 1629. Little action was taken until 1631 when Sandown Castle, which had been undermined by the sea, was dismantled by Sir John Oglander and a new defence was built to the north near Yaverland. It followed the now common rectangular plan with four arrow-head bastions. In the following year, in accordance with earlier recommendations, work was carried out at Yarmouth castle. This included the provision of internal accommodation for its gunners and the castle, with a small garrison, proved to be staunchly Royalist in the cause of Charles I.

THE CIVIL WARS

The Isle of Wight was fortunate in escaping the major rigors and upheavals of the Civil Wars (1642–51) and it prospered from this fact. Island rents and profits rose as many, chiefly gentry, arrived from the mainland to escape the troubles. The local land-owners were largely Royalist and Jerome Weston, 2nd Earl of Portland, who governed the island between 1633 and 1642, served the Crown in a number of capacities.

Carisbrooke was garrisoned by a small detachment of Royalist troops under Colonel Brett, but the mayor of Newport, a fanatical Puritan, was determined to seize the stronghold for the Parliament. When the besiegers advanced, the Countess of Portland, who had sought asylum in the castle, appeared on the ramparts with a lighted match and threatened to fire the first cannon and 'to hold the castle to the last extremity unless honourable terms of capitulation were granted'. The attacking force, ignorant of the fact that there were but three days' provisions left and that the defenders were nearly all invalided soldiers, thought it prudent to comply with the countess's demands. Carisbrooke, however, was obliged to capitulate to the Parliamentarians, and, in view of the island's loyalties, it was ruled briefly by a Committee of Safety composed of tradesmen. Puritanism and suspicion marked this rule in which free movement was greatly restricted. Philip Herbert, 4th Earl of Pembroke, and a Parliamentarian, was appointed as new governor (1642–47) to be replaced by Robert Hammond, whose year-long appointment is now regarded by many as part of a clever plot to trap and imprison the King.

In his struggle with Cromwell Charles was defeated in the field on 3 June 1647, and held under house arrest at Hampton Court Palace. Parliament insisted on constitutional government, but the King was convinced of his divine right to rule as an autocrat. Fearing imminent trial or assassination by extremists, Charles, with the aid of loyalist friends, escaped to Thames Ditton. Here he was joined by Sir John Berkeley and Colonel John Ashburnam, but their plans to reach and remain in Bishop Sutton in Hampshire were thwarted by the large number of Parliamentarians there. Charles's misguided decision to seek refuge in the Isle of Wight was greatly coloured by the fact that Robert Hammond was its Governor. Though a young man in his mid-twenties with a distinguished record as a Captain in the Parliamentary forces, Hammond had applied for this sinecure post, sacrificing for a time his military prospects. His motives, we are told, were apparently to gain quiet and to keep aloof from the violent measures to which

The rural scene: *(above)* Near Bembridge. The restored windmill, the property of The National Trust, is the sole survivor on the island; *(below)* agricultural land at St Catherine's Point with the famous lighthouse in the background *(British Tourist Authority)*

The 'Medusa Mosaic' at the Roman Villa, Brading *(British Tourist Authority)*

some of his colleagues were already openly committed.

Charles naturally thought Hammond would protect him for he was also the nephew of the King's chaplain at Hampton. Hammond, however, was also related to Cromwell by marriage and was reluctant to put his comfortable position at risk. 'His temptation', says Carlyle, 'when the King announced himself in his neighbourhood had been great. Shall he obey the King in this crisis; conduct the King witherward His Majesty wishes? Or be true to his trust and the Parliament?' When the King's messengers arrived, Hammond, in order to gain time to consult Parliament, volunteered to meet Charles at Titchfield where the King was in hiding. He was finally persuaded and in November 1647, Charles, attended by only three of his suite, accompanied the Colonel back to Carisbrooke.

In view of Hammond's close ties with Cromwell and the latter's unexplained visit to the island in September, there is a strong consensus of historical opinion that Charles I was deliberately manoeuvred into going to Carisbrooke which had been prepared as a royal prison. The King's decision to cross to the island was certainly curious, though perhaps the nearness of France, should exile be the last expedient, was the main attraction. The commentary on these events by Sir John Oglander summarises the local gentry's view of the King's arrival:

> King Charles came into our Island [on] Sunday the 14th November, to my great astonishment. For, as a great while I could not be brought to believe it, so, when I was certain of it I could do nothing but sigh and weep for two nights and a day. And the reason for my grief was that I verily believed he could not have come to a worse place for himself, or where he could be more securely kept. This being the chief [anxiety] yet I knew also it would be half an undoing to our poor Island, and I pray God I be no true prophet.

The Royal Prisoner

Charles was indeed a captive at Carisbrooke but initially he was treated as a royal guest and was given one of the best rooms

73

at the castle. He enjoyed ample liberty, was allowed to ride and hunt in Parkhurst Forest and the gentry of the island visited him for discussions and social evenings. The King's comforts were further improved by the shipment of furniture from the mainland which included luxurious beds and carpets and a stock of favourite books. Charles's table cost Carisbrooke the large sum of £10 a day and Hammond was assigned an allowance for defraying his household expenses.

Most of Charles's time at Carisbrooke, however, was spent in political scheming for he was determined to regain what he considered his full divinely ordained rights. A secret treaty with the Scots was signed in 1647 and, understandably, when news of it leaked out, Charles was no longer considered a 'guest' at Carisbrooke, but a dangerous prisoner. Ineffective escape attempts also led to his further confinement though the old 'Barbican' or parade ground of the castle was converted into a bowling green and a summer-house was erected for his enjoyment.

The escape plans were in true Hollywood style. The first was in February 1648˙ when a plot was devised by Richard Firebrace, his faithful servant. The plan was to break through the ceiling of the King's chamber, thereby passing above a number of rooms to a part of the castle unguarded by sentries. Not only Hammond, but the Derby House Committee in London were well aware of this attempt and it came to nought. The second escape was organised for 20 March when, alerted by pebbles thrown at his window, Charles was to squeeze through a small casement into an unguarded inner court, scale the castle wall by a rope and be met by friends with horses to convey him to a boat. In spite of Firebrace's concern Charles was convinced he could squeeze through the bars of the casement window. Inevitably he got stuck and with some difficulty was eased back into the room. 'I heard him groan', wrote Firebrace later, 'but could not come to help him, which (you may imagine) was no small affliction to me.' Charles was then moved to the quarters of the chief officer which were considered easier to guard, but his attempt to escape from here by bribing the sentry was equally amateurish for, inevitably, he was betrayed.

Charles was detained at Carisbrooke until the September following when the farcical 'Treaty of Newport' was signed between the House of Commons and the monarch. Under this he was allowed to live in comfort in Newport at the former King James I Grammar School. After a period of fruitless negotiations with representatives of Parliament he was moved across The Solent to Hurst Castle where he was imprisoned for two months before being transferred to London. In January 1649 he was tried by a court of 150 commissioners presided over by John Bradshaw, an eminent lawyer. In what is undoubtedly one of the most famous trials in English history, Charles I clung to his 'divine right' with a mixture of Stuart obstinacy and royal dignity, refusing either to enter a plea or to admit that the court was competent to try him. An entry in the register of Carisbrooke church records the melancholy sequel: 'In the year of our Lord God, 1649, January the 30th day, was Kinge Charles beheaded at Whitehall Gate.' His royal injunction from the scaffold was simply, 'Remember'.

In July of the following year two of the late King's children, Henry, Duke of Gloucester, and the Princess Elizabeth, were transferred from Penshurst, the historic home of the Sidneys, to Carisbrooke. On 8 September 1650, in her fifteenth year, the Princess died of a fever and was buried in Newport Church. 'As to the boy', Cromwell had bluntly said, 'it would be better to bind him to a trade.' Two years later, however, he was freed but died in Holland in 1660.

The Isle of Wight certainly 'remembers' Charles I, for his imprisonment and that of his children at Carisbrooke is one of the most notable incidents in the island's history. It is comparable, perhaps, to that period almost two hundred years later, when Victoria, another monarch proud of a Scottish ancestry, sought refuge and solace in the island. Not surprisingly the principal monument in St Thomas' Church, Newport, is that erected by Queen Victoria to Princess Elizabeth. Originally buried in the chancel of the old church, her resting place was forgotten until 1793, when some workmen stumbled upon the coffin. The monument commissioned by Victoria is executed in Carrara marble and is regarded as one of Marochetti's finest works. The likeness was from a portrait in the possession of the Queen and the broken iron bars above the monument are obviously symbolical. The inscription reads:

> To the memory of The Princess Elizabeth, daughter of King Charles I, who died at Carisbrooke Castle, on Sunday, September 8th, 1650, and is interred beneath the chancel of this church. This monument is erected as a token of respect for her virtues, and of sympathy for her misfortunes, by Victoria R. 1856.

THE RESTORATION

'From the time of the Restoration', states Lawrence Wilson in his *Portrait of The Isle of Wight*, 'recorded history dwindles off into the names of successive Governors, aristocrats who had little to do with the island, but were pleased enough to draw a salary of £1,000 a year which was not abolished until 1789 when the Governorship became purely honorary and the island was administered by local nominees.'

Following Charles I's removal from Carisbrooke and the Isle of Wight, nothing more is heard of Robert Hammond for there is no documentation of his resignation and not even a portrait survives, just a woodcut. The joint Governorship by Sydenham and Fleetwood, Cromwellian soldiers, deserves little comment, but with the return of Charles II the former Royalist Governor, Jerome Weston, returned to his post for a brief period, before resigning in favour of Thomas Culpeper (1661–70) who later became a Governor of Virginia.

Such figures are completely overshadowed by the romantic figure of Sir Robert Holmes, sailor, Royalist, buccaneer, semi-pirate, musketeer and Governor and Captain of the Isle of Wight from 1670 to 1692. A life-size statue of Holmes may be seen in the small vestry of Yarmouth Church, for he was the town's hero. Yet even the poorest judge of art will observe that the head and body are sculptured differently, for the former is ridiculously large to fit a body dressed in cavalier riding boots and flowing drapery. The unfinished statue was apparently intended to represent Louis XIV, and was being conveyed to Paris in order that the artist might model the head from the living subject. After capturing the French ship and appropriating the statue, Holmes compelled the artist to substitute his own features for those of *le Grand Monarque*. One version of the story states that this is the reason why Holmes's face wears a whimsical grin; the other maintains that the artist achieved his revenge by giving the Governor a sour expression! The tradition must be accepted, for it is one of the best tales told of Holmes, although there are numerous variations.

Holmes, however, was no comic, for he served the navy with dedication, making forays against the Dutch which together with France were currently England's political and commercial enemies. In 1663 he had captured, off the coast of Guinea, a Dutch vessel carrying gold which, apparently, was used in the manufacture of the first coinage to be given the name Guineas. The gold was so good that a pound's worth of it was equal to £1.1s. In the following year he took New Amsterdam and his naval career in Africa, America and the Baltic led to his knighthood and the founding of a family long dominant in the Isle of Wight. While Governor he reduced the size of Yarmouth's garrison and built a private residence adjacent to the castle, whose back premises, with its fine oak staircase and panelling, are now part of the George Hotel.

Subsequent Governors pale in comparison to Sir Robert Holmes, probably because the fears of invasion from the continent gradually subsided and the island returned to more domestic pursuits. The Dutch fleet had been sighted on a number of occasions but there was no action and following the defeat of the French at the Battle of La Hogue in 1692, the local militia were virtually disbanded and not recalled for a hundred years.

6   THE ANCIENT BOROUGHS

*Since my memory Newport was a very poor town, the
houses most thatched, the streets unpaved and in
the High Street, where now be fair houses, were
garden plots. The Bailies themselves were but
fishermen and oyster draggers—the meanest shop
now has far more wares than all the shops then had.*

Sir John Oglander, *Notebook*, 1632

LTHOUGH little has so far been said of Wight's
ancient boroughs they were intimately linked with the
island's political and economic vicissitudes, receiving in
particular the full impact of the French raids. Town
development, by southern English standards, appeared late for
in spite of their villas there is no evidence that the Romans
founded urban centres on the island and, whether it was a
reflection of insularity or a basic impoverishment of local
resources, no boroughs are mentioned in the *Domesday Book*.
Newtown, Yarmouth and Newport were founded as Norman
planned or planted towns, but the history of Brading is
somewhat different for it was established by Edward I when he
was in firm control of the island.

The Isle of Wight boroughs were founded primarily for
economic reasons—to reap advantages from a place where
building plots were let against money rents instead of rents in
kind—rather than as military centres for securing newly-
conquered or acquired lands. With costly wars to finance, the
initial success of the boroughs was undoubtedly a major factor

in Edward I's interest in the Isle of Wight, though their sustained growth was dependent on, and affected by, a number of factors. The resource potential of the hinterland they served, together with adequate communications, particularly by water, were obvious controls, but political events were of paramount importance and the wars with France revealed the slim, often precarious, economic and social bases of the Wight boroughs. Newtown, for example, never really recovered from the French raid of 1377 and Newport and Yarmouth, also sacked, suffered a long period of urban decline in which plague and pestilence further protracted urban renewal.

NEWTOWN

Historically, Newtown is the most interesting and, in all probability, the most ancient of the island's boroughs. In 826 its site formed part of the lands of Swainston, or Calbourne,

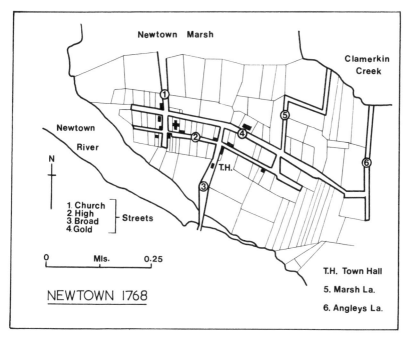

NEWTOWN 1768

Newtown Marsh

Clamerkin Creek

Newtown River

N

1. Church
2. High
3. Broad   } Streets
4. Gold

0   Mls.   0.25

T.H.

T.H. Town Hall
5. Marsh La.
6. Angleys La.

which had been given by Egbert of Wessex to the Bishops of Winchester. Within this manor they built a hall at Swainston which the *Domesday Book* records as being a normal rural manor with its main source of income coming from agricultural produce. The first reference to a borough charter is that granted by Aymer de Valance, Bishop Elect of Winchester, in 1256 and it was subsequently confirmed by Edward I and other monarchs. It referred to the founding of a 'new town' whose settlement seems to have existed under an earlier title of Franchville, indicating perhaps that it enjoyed earlier privileges and was free, or almost free, from manorial obligations. 'Know all ye men', began the Bishop's edict, 'that we have given to our Burgesses of the Borough which is called Franchville all the liberties and free customs which our Burgesses of Taunton, Witney, Alresford and Farnham have . . .' The new borough was variously known as Swainston, le Neuton (Newtown) or Francheville (Freetown), the latter names, like Neustadt, Villeneuve, Villefranche and Villafranca on the Continent, indicating the planned nature of its foundation.

Although today the Newtown River is largely silted up, the dominant factor in the borough's history was its location beside this estuary. In its heyday, Newtown harbour was capable of berthing the largest of English warships and it was this, together with the early success of its markets, that attracted Edward I. A bishop's territory, however, was not easy for the crown to acquire, but in 1284 Winchester was forced to relinquish the valuable manor and to pay dues to retain its other temporalities. At this date there were over seventy-seven burgages on Newtown's rent role and the burghal rights were worth about £29 a year. All that the Bishop retained was the advowson of the thirteenth-century village chapel of St Mary Magdalene, itself dependent on the church at Calbourne.

Newtown by the fourteenth century was a thriving community and was assessed at twice the value of Newport. The busy and important harbour was regarded as the most commodious and safest in the island and there were profitable

Carisbrooke Castle: *(above)* The twelfth-century Norman Keep with Elizabethan buildings in the old Bailey; *(below)* the thirteenth- and fourteenth-century gatehouse

(above) The restored Newtown Town Hall (1699) recalls the earlier glories of an ancient borough; *(below)* old warehouses at Newport Quay are reminders of the former significance of this town as a port

Yarmouth: *(above)* One of the busiest yacht harbours on the south coast, but still used by work boats *(British Tourist Authority)*;
(right) Yarmouth Castle. The original gateway surmounted by the Royal arms of Henry VIII. The crowned shield is supported by the lion and golden dragon

Island churches: *(top left)* St Mary's, Brading, was founded by Bishop Wilfrid and is allegedly the oldest church on the island; *(top right)* Gatcombe church. Mainly thirteenth century with a fifteenth-century tower; *(bottom left)* St Thomas's, Newport. A prominent nineteenth-century town church built on an earlier foundation oyster beds in the estuarine marshes and a flourishing salt industry where sea water was evaporated in great salterns. According to the ancient leases of the fisheries the tenant was obliged to provide oysters, as well as 'a good dish of fish' for the mayoral feast. Edward II's charter confirmed Newtown's privilege of a weekly market and that of a three-day fair, held on 'the eve, the day and the morrow of the Feast of St Mary Magdalene'.

The story of Newtown's decline parallels that of the other island boroughs. In 1377 the town was raided and burnt by the French and may have been only partially rebuilt. It could-still harbour part of the Armada fleet (and as late as 1781 the port could accommodate fifty vessels of 500 tons) but the borough had lost its former importance and in 1559 it was described as having 'streets bothe of artificers and others cleyn dekeyed'. Plague probably had a hand in devastating the town for there is a fourteenth-century legend analogous to Hamelin's Pied Piper which speaks of a plague of rats—the latter being an allegory for the Black Death or some other disease spread by vermin. The Elizabethan surveyors also attributed its decline partly to the removal of the wool staple from Winchester to Calais in the fourteenth century, which severely damaged the economy of Hampshire. Probably in an attempt to revitalise the borough Elizabeth I, in 1584, gave parliamentary representation to Newtown which continued to elect two members during the next 250 years. Its parliamentary career, however, came to an end in 1832 when it was declared a 'Rotten Borough' and was disenfranchised under the first Reform Act. In 1835, a Government Commission on Municipal Corporations reported that no burgesses resided in the borough and that there were no inhabitants 'capable of exercising any municipal function' or 'sufficient inhabitants of intelligence to make a court-leet jury'. Its fair, the 'Newtown Randy', had ceased; the Town Hall, built around 1700, became redundant and the inn and shops closed their doors.

John Mallet's plan of the borough in 1768, based on an earlier plan of the Manor of Swainston made in 1636, indicates only twelve inhabited buildings and a dilapidated chapel. Old burgage plots were aligned along both sides of the High Street and along the north side of Gold Street. Broad Street commenced at the stone bridge across the Newtown Creek and formed the stem of a double T-shaped plan, the cross-pieces being formed by the east and west sections of Gold and High Streets. The Town Hall stood in the middle of Broad Street and over forty descriptively named plots are shown, together with the remains of holdings in a common field. The salterns and fish-breeding ponds are also indicated.

These divisions can still be traced in Newtown's overgrown lanes, alleys and plots, but the Town Hall, restored by a group of anonymous benefactors, is the only real remaining monument to the borough's past importance. Though small, it is complete with Council Chamber or Courtroom, Robing Room and the Mayor's Parlour and contains an interesting collection of records, other documents and insignia relating to Newtown's history. To the north, on the corner of Broad and High Streets, is the old inn; above its doors is the coat of arms with the words 'S. Comatis: de Franchville de l'ile de Wight'.

YARMOUTH

Known in earlier times as Eremud or Eremue, Yarmouth received its first charter from Baldwin de Redvers, who, in 1135, granted the settlement 'all liberties and customs belonging to free Burgesses, and quittance from tolls and other customs in fairs and markets'. These privileges applied in all the lands and estates owned by him for, as previously stated, the de Redvers held large territories in south-west England as well as the Isle of Wight. With its own weekly market and annual fair Yarmouth developed as an important island town, but it was chiefly its strategic situation and harbour facilities that initially gave the borough greater significance than the mere number of inhabitants would seem to warrant. This, however, was to be its downfall for it was a primary target for enemy raiders in the Channel.

The town's early charter was confirmed in 1334 by Edward VI and then by a number of subsequent monarchs, but all these renewals and amendments to its borough status were not sufficient to counteract the devastation brought by the French raid of 1377. So badly was Yarmouth sacked that it was let off its taxes and it was again raided in the early sixteenth century. Henry VIII's newly-constructed fort, and the fact that for various periods it was the seat of the governor and captain of the island, did little to prevent its decline, and throughout the Elizabethan era there are descriptions and complaints of its decay. In 1559 it is reported that scarcely a dozen houses were left inhabited and a brief, dated 1611, called for the rebuilding of its church through public subscriptions:

> there remains only the ruinated chancell of one of its churches, and the town being unable from its own resources to erect and fit a decent church, the charitable devotion and liberal contribution of the King's loving subjects throughout the realm is requested towards the new building and re-edyfing (*sic*) of the said church at Yarmouth.

Thus the town's parish church is the third on the present site, the previous buildings having been destroyed by raiders.

The Reform Act of 1832 regarded Yarmouth as another 'Rotten Borough' and in 1883 its municipal corporation ceased to exist, with the settlement coming under the administration of a town trust of eleven members. Unlike Newtown, however, modern Yarmouth, chiefly because it is the terminus of the Lymington ferry, has again risen to the status of a town with a mayor and all municipal privileges. Its ancient town hall stands near the centre of a small, but regular grid-iron street plan which has changed little from the time of the borough's inception. Its four gates—Quay Gate, Outer and Inner Town Gates and Hither Gate—have long disappeared, but Yarmouth still retains a distinctive, even aloof atmosphere, the natural product of longevity.

BRADING

Brading was not a Norman foundation. The town's charter was first granted in 1280 by Edward I, but it appears to have belonged to the Crown from earlier times. In the twelfth century it formed part of the Manor of Wightfield which was crown property and its own coat of arms describes it as the 'Kyngs Towne of Brading'. Edward VI confirmed Brading's market rights and also those to hold two annual fairs, one for three days from 1 May and the other for two days from 21 September. By Elizabethan times it appears that Brading had developed a sense of civic pride unusual for the age. An entry in the Town Book indicates that its inhabitants were responsible for the paving of the main street and every householder was requested to clean their doors at least once a week. Sanitary consciousness was also beginning to stir for 'it was ordered . . . that none of the Town . . . shall carry into Halfpenny Lane any soil or dirt, nor otherwise to ease their bodies there'. The fine for committing such an Elizabethan nuisance was fourpence!

Brading's prosperity in the Middle Ages was related to its harbour for it was a significant south coast port and the area that is today Bembridge Harbour then extended inland for a mile and a half and was known as Brading Haven. Such creeks and river mouths, as at Newtown and Newport, were favourite town sites in earlier centuries, offering some form of protection from sea marauders yet furthering local fishing and commerce. Until 1880 small craft could ascend with the tide to Brading quay which can still be traced where houses in the old village line a bank of the river above the flood mark. At the end of the eighteenth century Brading was the largest centre in East Wight and was the regional testing-centre for weights and measures. It was to Brading that the inhabitants of the small fishing village of Ryde came for more specialist goods and services.

The harbour at Brading met the same fate as that at Newtown; it gradually silted up leaving the Yar to follow a circuitous course through meadows and marshlands. The first attempt to reclaim this area was made by a number of Dutch engineers appointed by Sir Hugh Myddleton during the reign of James I. It proved expensive and, ultimately, unsuccessful and it was not until 1878 that an embankment of more than a mile in length was constructed across the harbour mouth. Thus Brading was cut off from the sea, its market also became obsolete and by the end of the century its two fairs, held on Brading Down, were discontinued. It followed that the Corporation of Brading was dissolved but a trust was formed to administer the former borough's property.

Brading's appearance today is that of a large village (with villa extensions) whose principal street straggles a steep hill to the Church of St Mary. Adjacent is the small, greatly restored, Town Hall which contains relics of the borough's former glory and in the enclosed space or market-place beneath are the old stocks and whipping-post. At the Sandown end of the settlement is the old ring used for bull-baiting where, according to the Oglander MSS,

> it was the custom from time immemorial for the Governor of the Isle of Wight to give five guineas to buy a bull to be baited and given to the poor. The mayor and the corporation attended at the bull-ring in their regalia, with mace-bearers and constables; and after proclamation, a dog called the mayor's dog, ornamented with ribbons, was in their presence set at the bull.

NEWPORT

Although it is the island's historical capital, Newport fought hard for this distinction. It takes its origin from a charter by Richard de Redvers II in 1177, though it may have had an earlier foundation without special privileges. As its name indicates the borough was founded as a 'new port' (*Novus Burgus meus de Medina*) for Carisbrooke which was, and remained for some time, the governmental and administrative centre for the island. Newport was not given ecclesiastical independence and its church, until 1858, came under the jurisdiction of Carisbrooke and initially the monks of Carisbrooke Priory contracted to serve it. On early maps and plans the dependent status of the church is indicated by the absence of a graveyard and it seems that a plague was needed during the reign of Elizabeth I before funerals ceased to journey to Carisbrooke.

Newport developed primarily in relationship to its central position within the island and to its location at the head of the navigable part of the Medina. Early prosperity came from its harbour dues, manufacturing crafts and, above all, from its fairs and markets. In spite of its geographical advantages Newport suffered fierce competition from its rival boroughs and, like them, enemy raids, pestilence and financial difficulties led to long periods of economic stagnation and decline. In 1377, after sacking Yarmouth and Newtown the French, in the words of the Exchequer Records, proceeded to the 'entire burning, wasting and destroying of the town of Newport, so that no tenants were resident for upwards of two

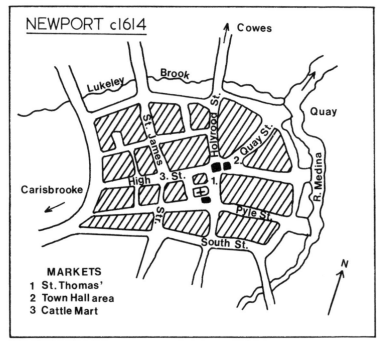

NEWPORT c1614

Cowes

Brook

Lukeley

St. James St.

Holyrood St.

Quay St.

Quay

High St.

3. St.

Carisbrooke

R. Medina

Pyle St.

South St.

N

MARKETS
1 St. Thomas'
2 Town Hall area
3 Cattle Mart

years'. There is no mention of Newport in the poll tax returns of 1378, but a record for 1379 indicates that its taxpaying population had been reduced to fifty-six inhabitants. By the reign of Edward VI (1547–53), however, 800 inhabitants are recorded but, when in 1559, a commission under the direction of Sir Francis Knollys was appointed to inquire into the borough's decay and speed up its redevelopment, the bailiffs and burgesses fatalistically blamed the town's condition on the French raid over 170 years earlier. Undoubtedly, the outbreak of pestilence in 1349 also played a part in Newport's protracted decline.

Visitations of the plague were not infrequent to medieval and early modern towns and between October 1583 and May 1584 Newport was ravaged by plague affecting around 300 people, many of whom died. God's Providence House, one of the architectural and historical treasures of the modern borough, is traditionally the site of the only house in which no one fell victim. In the second week of May only one person died and the borough archives record that 'the plage ceased, and God, of his mercy, toke ye plage from the Towne to our great comfertt, praysed be to his holy name'.

The old burial ground to the south of the town, formerly the archery green, was the outcome of this plague and its consecration on 23 May 1583 was the first step towards the emancipation from the church at Carisbrooke. Pestilence returned to Newport in 1621 and 1627, the former being smallpox brought from London, and when the Great Plague reached its full violence in London in 1665 the Isle of Wight was declared a protected area. In spite of strict measures to prevent the arrival of unauthorised persons from the mainland, the plague crossed The Solent and Newport was again badly hit. The local farmers were terrified to visit its markets and it is recorded that when Lady Richards of Yaverland, who had a town house in Newport, decided to return to Yaverland Manor to escape the pestilence, the villagers, most of them being her tenants, were determined to prevent her.

The Tudor commission of 1559 had suggested a number of

measures to help and assist the urban renewal of Newport, yet it appears that these were not acted upon. As Sir John Oglander indicated, it remained a poor town throughout the sixteenth century but in 1661 the burgesses were granted their final charter by Charles II which provided for the election of a mayor and the seventeenth-century growth of trade in south-coast towns led to a revival of Newport's prosperity.

Although its old buildings have sadly been removed the centre of Newport, in terms of its street pattern, is little changed from that depicted on John Speed's plan of the town in 1614, given as an inset to his map of the island. Within the physical limits of its site the plan of Newport seems to have followed the grid-pattern typical of many planned boroughs. Speed indicates five parallel streets running east to west with two central north–south streets. This regular grid was disrupted by the river estuary and by a broad street which ran from the market areas to the quay.

Speed's plan shows no gates, but an earlier plan of 1611 indicates a gate called Town Gate at the north side of St James Street and it is probable that other gates existed, though there is no evidence and certainly no proof of a wall.

The old town comprised three open spaces for trading and markets, the principal one being the Corn Market or St Thomas's named after the church which occupied the centre. On its north side was the flesh and fish shambles and on the west the market house which functioned as such until the nineteenth century when it became an inn. At the north-east stood the cheese cross which formed a connecting link with the open space at the junction of Quay, High and Holywood Streets. It is here that the Town Hall stood. The third open space was St James's beast market where the ring for bull-baiting probably stood and almost certainly this was a place for public punishment. This area still housed the town market until 1928 when it was moved to new yards on South Street. Continuity also exists in the site of the Town Hall, the new one having been built by Nash in 1816, and the narrow streets around the quay have changed little over the centuries.

(above) Outside the Royal Yacht Squadron clubhouse on the site of West Cowes
Castle. In the background is the Southampton ferry *(British Tourist Authority)*;
(below) the chain ferry across the Medina linking East and West Cowes

Queen Victoria: the memorial to Queen Victoria in St James's Square, one of Newport's old market areas; *(below)* the Queen's bedroom at Osborne – her favourite home *(British Tourist Authority)*

7 TRADITIONAL LIVELIHOODS

Its fertility is almost proverbial
having long since been said to produce
more in one year than could be consumed
by the inhabitants in eight.

Rev Warner, 1794

THE urban renewal of Newport, following its long period of stagnation and decline, was a natural reflection of the island's improved economic and social status, for town and country, especially in an insular setting, were closely linked. Periods of either prosperity or depression in the one were reciprocated or reflected in the other and undoubtedly Newport's protracted condition was as much related to enemy raids, pestilence and general poverty in the countryside as it was to its own difficulties. Newport, however, was more than a market town for the countryside, for its port facilities played an important role in fusing two complementary lifestyles, one which gained a living from the land and the other that looked to the sea for sustenance. Newport's status as a provincial capital had been constantly challenged in the past and again it was to suffer competition from expanding island communities, especially from the small, but dynamic port of Cowes which from the seventeenth century onwards handled an ever-increasing proportion of the island's trade goods.

The inhabitants of Cowes, both East and West, had always been seafarers and traders, or at least smugglers. On the west side of the Medina the early 'port' was higher up the river at the Shamblers, but in the early seventeenth century a quay for handling imported goods was erected at East Cowes which not only took the place of the Shamblers but also prejudiced the position of Newport. An important trade developed with the American Colonies and the Custom House Books record that Cowes in 1677 imported 4,000 hogsheads of tobacco from Virginia as well as other goods from America and Holland. Cowes was also an important transhipment port for cargoes destined for the continent, chiefly Holland and Germany. A plaque on the modern Parade indicates the close association of Cowes with America. It was erected by the State of Mayland in 1933 to commemorate the three-hundredth anniversary of Leonard Calvert and his co-adventurers who sailed in the *Ark* and the *Dove* to establish the Palatinate of Maryland under a charter granted by Charles I, which conferred upon its people all the rights of Englishmen. These are rights that Maryland still cherishes as its most valuable heritage.

Yet the port of Newport managed to survive the competition of expanding Cowes as its nineteenth-century warehouses, mills and wharves would indicate. Though never the scene of marine congestion the quays are still alive with old barges and cargo boats with loads of timber, gravel and grain. Around 1800 the latter was Newport's chief export and the staple of the island: 'vast quantities of grain . . . are sent down from hence to Cowes—not less than two hundred wagon loads of different sorts of grains were formerly brought to every market, part of which was made into flour and malt, and the remainder brought up for exportation'. Such production, although there were times when grains were less profitable, remained in the hands of the local gentry and landowners, whose estates with their large manor houses could be traced back to Domesday times and beyond.

THE GENTRY AND THE LAND

Throughout most of the eighteenth century, rural Wight was

quietly prosperous and in 1748 it had received Daniel Defoe's special commendation for its fertile, well-cultivated land, and for the fine quality of its wool. Yet from the farm labourers' point of view it was not quite 'the paradise of England' that Sir John Oglander had described a century earlier. Any fluctuations in prices, leading to changes in land-use management, affected the farm hands first who in Defoe's time got little more than a few shillings weekly. Even by the 1830s a farm hand raised only nine shillings a week and boys earned sixpence a day. The wages of domestic servants were also extremely low.

Seen through the eyes of the gentry, island life would certainly have appeared attractive and leisurely; at least twice a week local squires would meet on St George's Down, west of Arreton manor, to play bowls and then to dine in a local club house. On Saturday afternoons as many as 'thirty knights and gentlemen' would meet again at an 'ordinary' in Newport for further relaxation. Though fox-hunting was not a popular sport until the end of the eighteenth century, fishing, particularly sea fishing off the southern coast, was another favourite pastime and archery was again becoming fashionable. This reached its greatest popularity in the nineteenth century when old target fields were revived and archery fêtes were held, rather reminiscent perhaps, of the current island craze in inns and clubs for the diminutive dart which is thrown in challenge matches throughout the island and on organised excursions to the mainland.

The gentry consisted of old island families (like the Oglanders whose ancestors arrived with the Norman Conquest) and newer landowners from the mainland such as the Worsley family. As previously stated the Civil Wars had left the Isle of Wight politically and socially undisturbed and it became something of a haven for rich 'refugees' from the mainland. Thus, over the centuries, land was inherited, bought, sold, dowered and exchanged, processes which led to a profusion of manor and other country houses, many tracing their origins to Anglo-Norman times and invariably associated with a village community and parish church, thus preserving the traditional manorial pattern of organisation.

The size of these estates varied considerably but the tendency was for the largest and oldest to be located south of the central ridge on the Chalk and Greensand areas, where a combination of cereal cultivation and sheep rearing—the island's wool was noted for its quality—produced large but variable profits. These profits were often used, particularly at the beginning of the eighteenth century, to alter and extend manor and country houses. Thus Arreton, Nunwell, Yaverland, Apse, Stenbury, Morton, Wolverton, Mottistone, Merston, Sheat and others, provide examples of well-preserved Elizabethan and Jacobean houses, built of local stone and many of them are set in areas of unspoilt scenery. A large number of the island's farms are of similar pedigree.

Though some of the island's country houses have been converted into flats or put to other uses, Nunwell House is one of the few still occupied by a landed family. Situated three-quarters of a mile west of Brading, this is the ancestral home of the Oglander family, which, until the extinction of the male line with the death of the 7th baronet in 1874, could trace its lineage directly to Richard d'Oglandres who attended William Fitz Osborn at the Conquest. The name connection persists and the Oglanders are still undoubtedly the best known of all Wight families. The house is an early Tudor construction with an added Georgian façade and the first part of it was built at the time of Sir John Oglander, the historian and diarist. He died in 1655, but the published extracts of his private memoirs provide fascinating insights of the Isle of Wight's role within England as a whole. Nunwell House itself is rich in historic and dramatic events. Henry VIII was a guest of the family and Charles I dined at Nunwell when detained at Carisbrooke. The house survives today as a three-storeyed building of a number of architectural styles, surrounded by extensive parks and gardens.

The majority of Elizabethan and Jacobean houses tended to follow the standard E- or H-plans which are represented on the

Isle of Wight by such houses as Yaverland, Wolverton and Arreton. One reaction against this style is Appuldurcombe House, near Wroxall, which is a masterpiece of English Baroque architecture. It was begun by Sir Robert Worsley in 1710 to replace the old Tudor manor-house, but in 1943 it was the direct target of a German mine and its shell is now protected by the Ministry of Works. Sir Nicholas Pevsner's description of the house places it in its true architectural context:

> with its fine ashlar work, its square centre and low angle pavilions, its array of giant pilasters and its dramatic twin chimneys on the four corners, it is Baroque in the English sense without any doubt, but it is highly personal and has not so far been attached convincingly to any architect's *oeuvre*.

Gatcombe House was another seat of the Worsley family and was intended as a smaller and less pretentious edition of Appuldurcombe House. Standing in a rich park with plane trees, it was built by Sir Edward Worsley in 1756 though its Palladian façade hides parts that are older. Latterly it belonged to the Seely family a member of which, Sir Charles Seely, in 1904 started the library service. His name is still connected with the libraries of the island. This part of the island is rich in historic houses for to the south of Gatcombe is Sheat manor and beyond, Chillerton and Billingham manors.

The Rev Warner's *General View of the Agriculture of the Isle of Wight* provides a useful, if superficial and slightly biased, picture of island conditions in 1794. Like the reports prepared for the rest of England and Wales this one was compiled for the Board of Agriculture in order to meet the exigencies of the Napoleonic Wars when Britain needed to be self-sufficient in agricultural produce. Once again the island suffered the age-old fear of invasion and its population, which numbered around 20,000, was called to raise a defensive force from its main towns of Newport, Cowes and Yarmouth and from its thirty parishes. In July 1797, the Newport 'Volunteers' consisted of of 489 infantry with less than half that number of firearms. The island as a whole had 3,000 inhabitants under arms and it is recorded that 4,500 troops were brought over from the mainland. This meant a density of roughly one soldier to every three civilians. The island was one great garrison, but although enemy raiders intercepted vessels off the coasts, there was no French invasion.

According to Warner, the island's chief crops were the grains – wheat, barley and oats. The last-named occupied the 'stiff' lands and was grown in various rotations with clover. Beans, peas, turnips and potatoes were also cultivated, though potatoes were essentially a crop of the small farmer and agricultural labourer. According to reports the island potato was of excellent quality and a number of pleas and suggestions were made to increase its acreage in order to feed the Portsmouth market.

Sheep, mainly of the Dorset breed, were profitable animals and were well integrated into the island's system of husbandry which partly followed the 'Norfolk' pattern. An average of 40,000 sheep were shorn annually and 'last year', states Warner, '5,000 lambs were sold to London butchers . . . and in August, when I happened to be in Newport, one of these dealers bought 1,500 at a single purchase'.

The island's cows were of mixed breeds but produced good yields of milk which provided rich cream and butter. The local cheeses, however, were not popular with Warner, especially the variety called 'Isle of Wight Rock' which was extremely hard and could 'scarcely be cut by a hatchet or saw . . . masticated only by the firmest teeth and digested but by the strongest stomachs'.

Of all the agricultural improvements and innovations, the one which appealed to Warner the most was Sir Richard Worsley's determined effort to grow vines on a two-and-a-half acre site at St Lawrence. Taking advantage of the Undercliff's mild and sunny climate, vines native to western France were planted in 1792 and Breton workers were hired to tend them. Another plantation was added a year later making a total of

700 plants. A light wine was apparently produced from the White Muscadine and Plant Verd, but when interested parties arrived in 1808 the vines had been pulled up and replaced by more orthodox lawns. Whether it was the quality of the wine that led to this or the fact that Frenchmen were employed on English soil has not been substantiated.

QUARRIES AND CRAFTS

Although agriculture remained the economic pivot of the eighteenth century there were a number of extractive and craft industries that either supplemented agricultural wages or provided alternative forms of employment. Poor communications, however, both with the mainland and within the island restricted manufacturing development, and as late as 1791 Marshall remarked in *The Rural Economy of the Southern Counties* that 'there was not a turnpike road in the island unless between Newport and Cowes'.

The island had a good reputation for building stone, which in the case of the Bembridge and Binstead limestones had been worked from Roman times, and the rights to quarry them were sanctioned by the Norman kings. On either side of The Solent these stones had been used in churches and manor houses and also in a number of Henry VIII's forts. There were other good stone quarries, both inland and along the south coast, particularly in the Upper Greensand series where the outcrop of the 'freestone' is marked by a line of ancient quarries.

Much of the better and more accessible stone was worked out before the sixteenth century, but the Isle of Wight was richly provided with raw materials for brickmaking such as the Wealden shales, the Lower Greensand clays and also the Gault Clay. Other extractive industries included the quarrying of chalk for use on the land, and sands, thousands of tons of which were shipped to the glassworks in Bristol and Birmingham in the eighteenth and nineteenth centuries. There was some local glassmaking of very modest proportions and pottery was also a traditional craft.

101

Of the non-extractive industries tanning was of considerable importance and the monks of Quarr Abbey had earlier enjoyed high profits from their tanners. There was also a domestic cloth industry and at Newport starch and hair powder were manufactured on an extensive scale. The duty on flour used in the latter amounted to more than £3,000 in one year in the eighteenth century. But Newport's most notable industry was lace-making which by the end of the century employed 200 women and children, though it was nineteenth-century royal patronage that led to its real popularity, especially when the Princess Royal, on the occasion of her first appearance at court, in May 1856, wore a trimming of Newport lace on her train.

The trade directory of 1830 lists four lace-makers, two in Pyle Street, one at Coppins Bridge, and the most important, Nunn's Lace Manufactory at Broadlands. Nunn was a Nottingham banker whose interest in textiles led him financially to back a revolutionary lace-making machine invented by Brown and Freeman. Fearing local imitation, the initial firm split into two, one half going to Tewkesbury and the other to Newport. Nun's lace became famous in Europe and America for its beautiful and delicate designs, which were especially pleasing to Queen Victoria. When the Tewkesbury factory was closed in 1853 it was decided to concentrate all the work in Newport. At its busiest the factory had employed around 700 workers but by 1901 only a few old ladies were left.

THE SEA TRADES

Although Warner praises the benevolence of the Isle of Wight landowners and stresses, rather naïvely, the contentment of their workers, a considerable proportion of the island's population, either of economic necessity or with an eye to quick profits, gained some sort of income away from the land in sea or coastal trades. Rather curiously, fishing as an industry fails to feature prominently in the Isle of Wight's history, though an exception was the importance of its oysteries which had been famous from an early date. The main island beds were found at

Wootton Creek, the Medina estuary and Newtown River; the last, in particular, developed a wide reputation for its crop. Another important and highly lucrative coastal trade was the evaporation of salt from sea water, an industry which dated at least to the early twelfth century when Richard de Redvers confirmed to Quarr Abbey a tithe of all the salt produced at Lymington. Old salterns or saltpans fringe the island's estuaries and in the eighteenth century, when salt duties were sometimes as much as thirty or forty times the value of the product, large quantities were exported to London and elsewhere. Yet the island's most profitable trade, and at the same time its most unorthodox, was smuggling.

Smuggling

Smuggling as a profession was obviously not a legitimate maritime enterprise but, around the shores of Britain, it enjoyed a long and prosperous period. From its dawn down to the beginning of the nineteenth century it consisted of the more or less open landing of cargoes of contraband on beaches or in small havens. This 'free-trade' came to an end immediately after the French Wars when there was coastal blockading and after 1831 the coastguard and excise officials became organised on modern lines. On the island smuggling is of great antiquity and one of the earliest commodities in the trade was long staple English wool which was in great demand on the continent. Substantial profits were gained from the sale of fleeces directly to the Low Countries rather than to the mainland and the latter's woolsacks, via the Isle of Wight, also formed part of the trade.

By the eighteenth century smuggling rings operated from both coastal and inland settlements and the landowners were also involved, frequently financing profitable ventures. There was no shortage of hands: farm labourers during the eighteenth and early nineteenth centuries could earn more in one successful 'run' than they were paid in a week for long hours of farmwork. Although it is uncertain whether there was a 'Black Gang', the area around St Catherine's Point from Chale to

Niton, was a major centre for the smuggling trade, as, in fact, was the Undercliff in general, partly because of its extreme isolation. Other rings operated from Bembridge, St Helens, Sandown, Shanklin, Ventnor, and further west, from Atherfield, Brook and Freshwater. The difficulties experienced by customs officers in supervising this dangerous coast with its small, wild inlets, explains the role it played in the smuggling trade, as does its nearness to France from which most of the illicit cargoes were obtained.

Ships had been built at Cowes since the Middle Ages, but the smuggling trade led to a rapid expansion in shipbuilding. During the eighteenth century, smugglers, who required fast vessels disguised as fishing boats, frequently had them constructed at White's Yard. This firm had taken over Nye's Yard in the seventeenth century and specialised in naval craft. Ingenious methods of concealment were built into boats such as *Industry* (1827), and *Emulation* (1832), both built at Cowes, and the *Hold On* (1852) of Ryde. The success of White's boats, in particular, led to orders from customs officials for fast revenue cutters and by 1824 they owned boats which were efficient enough to apprehend smuggling vessels.

Sidney Dobell, the nineteenth-century poet, stayed at Niton for four successive winters and though he mistakenly calls St Catherine's Point 'the most southern nose of Great Britain', he was well aware of its smuggling industry. He wrote:

> Everyone has an ostensible occupation but nobody gets his money by it or cares to work in it. Here are fishermen who never fish but always have pockets full of money: and farmers whose farming consists of 'ploughing the deep' by night, and whose daily time is spent in standing, like herons, on look-out posts.

Dobell might have had in mind Ralph Stone of Niton, now a legendary character, who by night was a smuggler but by day cut a fine figure as a gentleman farmer dressed in velvet shooting coat and waistcoat, white hat, fancy breeches and Wellington boots.

Brandy, silk and tobacco, because they were heavily taxed, were the most profitable contraband items. Brandy could be purchased cheaply from France, chiefly Cherbourg, and was rowed or sailed back to the island under cover of darkness. A keg of brandy sold for fifty shillings on the mainland but could be purchased for fourteen shillings in Cherbourg. It was a colourless liquor and too far above the proof state to be drinkable, so it was diluted by the addition of water and caramel or brown sugar, which resulted in twice the profits. Ground herbs or rose-bush leaves were added to tea for the same purpose.

The local customs men, of course, were very active and great ingenuity was involved in concealing illicit goods and in their subsequent disposal. Brandy casks were often hidden in false-bottomed or false-sided boats, or they were weighted and dropped overboard at a pre-arranged spot to be retrieved later with grappling hooks or located by a 'peep tub'. This was a sawn-off tub which, when held over the side of a boat on the surface of shallow water, enabled the holder to view the bottom; a later refinement was the glazed-bottom tub. It was also known for brandy casks to be left on beaches covered in plaster to resemble a chalk cliff fall. Tobacco was also cleverly concealed and sometimes it was spun into imitation tarred rope and used as light rigging.

Once retrieved the movement of the contraband had to be efficient, quick and secretive. This was accomplished on foot, on horseback or in carts in which the goods were covered with farm produce, sometimes even dung. There were many hiding places en route such as woods, caves, cellars in farm and manor houses, ploughed fields and haystacks, any place in fact to trick the authorities. Many of the island's ghost stories were perpetuated by the smuggling fraternity to ward off the curious. As most goods were destined for the mainland it was a question of geography that made Rookley, near the centre of the island, the natural gathering and collecting place from coastal receipt points. On the mainland, Poole harbour was a favourite landing place for contraband.

Many islanders grew extremely rich from smuggling and one, by the name of Boyce, is described by Henry Fielding in his *Voyage to Lisbon*. Boyce, formerly a Gosport blacksmith, had built a large villa near Ryde named Apley House, where he lived in some style. Although he was practically illiterate he installed a library by ordering second-hand books worth £500 from a London dealer. When finally convicted of smuggling he was said to have had £40,000 in investments although, according to Fielding, his books raised very little at a Portsmouth auction 'for the bookseller ... relying on Mr Boyce's finding little time to read, had sent him not only the most lasting wares of his shop, but duplicates of the same, under different titles'.

That smuggling families could rise in society is illustrated by the now famous story of Sophie Dawes of St Helens. She was the daughter of a smuggler and oyster fisherman who was sent, on the death of her father, to work for a farmer. This was not to the thirteen-year-old girl's liking and she left for higher things, graduating through a number of 'situations' to become the mistress of the Duke of Kent. Sophie was lost in a game of cards to the Duc de Bourbon who took her back to France where she lived in almost regal splendour. Her entire St Helen's family joined her in the palace and Sophie Dawes eventually returned to England to die a very rich woman.

Shipwrecks
The bad reputation of the island's southern coast has been perpetuated by its numerous shipwrecks and other disasters. The first recorded incident was in 1314 when a vessel drove ashore on the infamous Atherfield Ledge in Chale Bay. It was part of a fleet carrying a consignment of wine from the King's Duchy of Aquitaine to England. The sailors escaped and sold the cargo locally, including fifty-three casks to Walter de Godeton, Lord of the Manor of Chale. Proceedings against the receivers of the stolen cargo followed and Godeton was fined 227 marks. Because the wine had belonged to a religious house Godeton was also ordered to build on St Catherine's Hill,

above the scene of the disaster, a lighthouse to warn ships and an oratory for a monk to trim the light and to recite masses for those lost at sea. The lighthouse was in operation until the dissolution of the monasteries but it was hardly effective for the persistence of fogs obstructed its light. Its remains today form a 35ft tower known locally as the 'Pepper Pot' and adjacent is the 'Salt Cellar', a 1785 lighthouse that proved equally abortive.

Over one hundred ships were wrecked in the area of Chale Bay between 1750 and 1850, one of the most notable the *Clarendon* in October 1836. The loss of nearly all her company stirred some reaction for the construction of a lighthouse close to the shore and the site chosen was the southernmost tip of the island, St Catherine's Point. It was completed in 1840, but its initial height of 120ft meant that fog obscured its light. It was subsequently reduced to 86ft and has been in service ever since, except during World War II when it proved too useful a guide to enemy planes. In 1858, the construction of the 80ft Needles lighthouse increased the protection around the south coast but, even so, there have been other wrecks in this area including the *Cormorant* in 1886 and the *Sirenia* in 1888, both off the Atherfield Ledge.

Wrecks, of course, could prove advantageous for the locals who were not adverse to helping themselves to any cargo that was washed ashore. There are many stories of 'professional' wreckers operating off the shores of southern England and the Isle of Wight, but few cases have been authenticated and most are the inventions of nineteenth-century novelists.

NEWPORT SOCIETY

The role of Newport in the island's late eighteenth and early nineteenth-century life is of considerable interest for not only did it function as a typical provincial capital and market town, it also heralded some of the social changes that were soon to affect the island. Newport's corn and cattle dealers controlled much of the island's farm produce and its lawyers and notaries handled the often complex affairs of the island's estates. The town's merchant entrepreneurs were involved with wool, lace and other trades and also with imports and exports, legal and otherwise. Newport's central position in an island where roads were still narrow rutted lanes, accounted for its economic importance.

Socially, too, Newport was a lively town and many of the country gentlemen had town houses there. Its attractions included dramatic performances, a periodical assembly, routs, reviews and even duels when someone's honour was at stake. On market days, in particular, Newport's streets were crowded with people and carts and an interesting, if patronising, diary entry of Mrs Philip Powys mentions its Saturday market which apparently attracted all classes.

> We made a party for the Saturday morning to meet at Newport market, a very fashionable rendezvous, to see the farmers' daughters, so much talked of for their beauty and neatness. When we got to that pretty town it seemed all the smarts of the island were assembled. The beauties aforementioned came on horseback with their baskets. They have a room where they now dress, and we are told a hairdresser always attends . . .

What precisely Mrs Powys was hinting at in this last sentence is not clear, but certainly with pretty girls and the presence of the 10th Regiment, which was quartered in Newport in 1799, the town must have been very lively. The Albany Barracks, named after the Duke of York and Albany, and now part of the Parkhurst Prison Complex, furnished accommodation for about 2,000 men.

Newport's increasing social life was reflected in some new buildings. The Isle of Wight Institution and the Guildhall, both built by Nash in the early years of the nineteenth century, are modest examples of ornate town architecture. By this time the island families were enjoying Newport's life to the full with, of course, the inevitable gossip and rumour that characterised a society where decorum was the thing. A letter to Henry Oglander in India from his sister, dated October 1837, reveals something of the problems of small-town existence, for apparently, one young lady 'astonished the ladies of Carisbrooke by appearing there in what she called her "Undercliff costume", which was a dress of *brown cloth*, which on a hot day must have been very uncomfortable and not quite so clean and nice either. She will not be a favourite if she takes so little care of her appearance in this smart island'.

VICTORIAN DISCOVERY

> *Drove down to the beach with my maids and went into*
> *the bathing machine, where I undressed and bathed*
> *in the sea (for the first time in my life). I*
> *thought it was delightful till I put my head under*
> *the water, when I thought I should be stifled.*

Queen Victoria, 30 July 1847

THE nineteenth-century discovery of the Isle of Wight as a pleasure, health and retirement centre was related in part to the general social revolution created by the growth of a rich middle class. Great profits were made during and after the Napoleonic Wars and the repeal of the Orders in Council, which had strangled trade with Europe, provided many professional people and manufacturers with even greater financial rewards. Landowners, too, reaped major advantages for the wars with France (and later America) decreased imports of European foodstuffs and gave home producers a prosperous monopoly, with the high prices and high rents continuing at least until the repeal of the Corn Law in 1846.

Although the upper echelon of society continued to take whole families on the Grand Tour, the early years of the nineteenth century saw the development of English watering places, particularly along the south coast, which catered for the growing middle class demand for sea air, bathing and leisure activities. The Isle of Wight's extensive coastline and profusion of safe and often secluded beaches was undoubtedly an important factor in its Victorian popularity as was its insular

(above) Appuldurcombe House, the island's sole Palladian mansion of which only the shell survives today; *(below)* the beach area at Ventnor

(*above*) The pier at Shanklin, one of the watering places that grew up along the coast in Victorian times; (*below*) Union Street, Ryde, is the town's commercial artery. Its steepness provides unique views of Solent ships (*IOW Tourist Board*)

character which appealed then, as now, to visitors who looked for something different. The pursuit of romantic scenery and the picturesque was also in vogue and the island offered inspiration to poets, artists and writers, just as its wealth of geological, botanical and archaeological interests attracted the more scientifically minded.

It was royal patronage and medical opinion that, together, transformed the Isle of Wight into one of Victorian England's most prestigious resorts. The founding of the Royal Yacht Squadron popularised Cowes and around 1830 the publication of books and papers by eminent physicians on the beneficial qualities of the island's climate and on the general curative properties of sea water led to the spectacular growth of small fishing settlements into famous coastal resorts. The picture of Queen Victoria being lowered in her bathing machine down a sloping pier into Osborne Bay is not the most orthodox image that is presented of this petulant, often domineering, monarch. Yet she had obviously been influenced by the researches of the Lewes practitioner, Dr Richard Russell, who upheld the iodine virtues of marine water and sea air as a cure of all ills. The Queen had built Osborne House, near East Cowes, as a private retreat, and this in itself led to that particular and fashionable Victorian cult of following in the footsteps of the royal family. Knowledge that Queen Victoria was a sea bather must certainly have popularised the beaches at Ryde, Ventnor and elsewhere on the island.

A PLACE IN THE COUNTRY

Three years after her accession to the throne in 1837 Queen Victoria married Prince Albert of Saxe-Coburg and together they began to consider the possibility of using part of their private incomes to purchase or build a house where they and their family could spend secluded vacations. The Queen already possessed Buckingham Palace, Windsor Castle and the Royal Pavilion at Brighton, but although well enough adapted for court ceremonial, they were found unsuitable for the privacy of a growing family. As Princess Victoria she had visited and liked the Isle of Wight, having stayed at Norris Castle outside East Cowes, and between 1839 and 1843 there was a strong possibility that the royal family might have bought it. Built in a mock-medieval style by James Wyatt towards the end of the eighteenth century, the castle suited Victoria's vision of 'a place of one's own, quiet and retiring' away from 'the fierce light that beats upon the throne', but its owners, the Seymour family, demanded too much money. The Queen's searches were directed to the adjoining Osborne House and estate owned by Lady Isabella Blanchford and after a trial visit the sale took place in March 1844. 'It is impossible to imagine a prettier spot', Victoria wrote, 'we have a charming beach quite to ourselves—we can walk anywhere without being followed or mobbed.'

The existing house proved to be too small and it was decided to rebuild it in two stages with a pavilion for the royal family and a big adjoining block for visitors and courtiers. The former was completed by 1846 and the household wing was largely finished by 1848. The designer was the artistic Prince Consort himself who enlisted the practical advice of Thomas Cubitt, a distinguished builder rather than an architect, who had developed much of Bloomsbury and almost all of Belgravia. Albert greatly admired the art and architecture of Italy and he saw in the view over The Solent a resemblance to the Bay of Naples. His design, which used the latest construction methods with cast iron beams, was thus an enlarged version of an Italian villa with tall towers or campaniles and a first-floor balcony or loggia. Though large, Osborne was deliberately designed as a house and not a palace and it became one of the best known, most illustrated and most imitated styles in the world with its popularity extending to America and the Colonies. In England, the 'Osborne style' was repeated, rather diminutively, in town halls, country houses, railway stations, suburban villas and seaside hotels.

In front of the house mock Renaissance terrace gardens adorned with fountains, balustrades and statues, led down to the sea and the grounds were filled with oaks, ash and cedars. Lewis Gruner, Prince Albert's artistic adviser, was consulted on this layout and also on the interior decoration, which was particularly elaborate. Both the state and private apartments, in true Victorian style, became littered with antiques, gifts and souvenirs of a lifetime, though Victoria's and Albert's private rooms were modestly furnished. The house had no central heating, because it was intended as a summer residence.

The Queen's happiness was tragically cut short by the death of Prince Albert in 1861 and for the next forty years she was in almost permanent residence at Osborne. Throughout her widowhood she endeavoured to keep every possible feature of the house and grounds unaltered, as being sacred to Albert's memory. The addition of the Durbar room was one exception. This was a large hall built on a former lawn on which a marquee had been erected for receptions that were too large to be held in the state apartments. The Indian style of decoration was chosen in honour of the Queen's possessions in India, of which she had been declared Empress in 1876. Its design was prepared by John Lockwood Kipling, father of the famous writer, and the work was executed under the direction of Bhai Ram Singh, an expert in Indian decorative techniques, particularly plasterwork. The Durbar room housed many rich caskets containing ceremonial addresses and other items commemorative of the Jubilees of 1887 and 1897.

Queen Victoria entertained most of the visiting royalty of the world at Osborne, as well as the leading members of the establishment. She died there on 22 January 1901 and Edward VII, who in any case spent much of his leisure time at Sandringham and had had unhappy visits at Osborne, promptly gave it to the nation. The royal apartments are open to the public; the rest is a convalescent home for officers.

RYDE AND ITS PIER

Although Victoria's presence at Osborne greatly affected the growth, style and atmosphere of Ryde, its initial development was due to the Player family who, at the beginning of the eighteenth century, acquired part of the manor of Ashey and began to lay it out in building plots. Henry Player built a mansion for himself close to the shore and a house was built on the quay on the site of the Old Watch House, afterwards known as the Black Horse Inn. A chapel, consecrated in 1719, was erected by Thomas Player and by 1756 the old quay, which had fallen into a dilapidated state, was rebuilt under the direction of a consortium of influential island gentlemen. Judging by the novelist Fielding's experiences that same year, this was a necessary undertaking for he states that the area 'between the sea and the shore was, at low water, an impassable gulf . . . of deep mud which could neither be traversed by walking or swimming so that for nearly one-half of the twenty-four hours Ryde was inaccessible by friend or foe'.

Not that there was a great deal to see in eighteenth-century Ryde for it consisted of two hamlets separated by fields called Node Close. The upper part was residential and was described by Hassal in 1789 (*Tour of the Isle of Wight*) as a 'plain, neat village with several well-built houses'. Lower Ryde was occupied by the cottages of fishermen and mariners and the settlements were linked by two packways, one becoming modern Ryde's Union Street, which was laid out in 1780 in relation to adjacent building plots.

By the turn of the century, Ryde, with its bracing climate, was becoming a popular watering place and lodging houses for the accommodation of visitors, together with private villas, were built in Union Street and in George and Nelson Streets, which ran parallel. Its 600 inhabitants in 1795 increased to 1,000 in 1801, to 1,600 in 1811 and to 3,000 in 1821.

There are some conflicting opinions on Ryde's early nineteenth-century development and appearance. An islander's account for 1831, though praising the character of Union Street, which 'was improving every day by new shops with large bow windows', was disturbed by the town 'continually expanding with badly built houses particularly to the east'. In 1838 these same houses were described as 'more resembling a slice of second-rate fashionable London stuck on the side of the island than anything which one would be prepared to meet with'. Sheridan was obviously enamoured of the people of position who were settling in the town for in 1834 he wrote that 'within the last few years houses of very superior description have been built both for permanent use and as desirable winter residences'. He quotes as examples the homes of the Duke of Buckingham, Earl Spencer, Lord Vernon, Sir Robert Simeon, the Honourable Charles Anderson, and others. Ryde, in fact, long before Bournemouth developed, was a chosen resort of the élite and the large family mansions in various parts of the town remain as memorials to this era.

The main impetus for development came in 1824 when the passenger pier was constructed and two years later the regular ferry service to Portsmouth commenced. At low tide, as Fielding had observed, nearly a mile of beach extends from the shore to the edge of the sea and before the pier was built passengers for the mainland were loaded on to horse-drawn carts which were taken through the shallow water to the waiting boats. The pier, which was extended and altered many times, was to make Ryde a main gateway to the island, firmly establishing it as a resort town and, with sand replacing mud, its flat beach was ideally suited for the use of the bathing machine. Speculative building was in full swing by the 1840s when 'many genteel families', as earlier guide books put it, 'were attracted to Ryde on account of the island's royal residence'. Miniature Osbornes sprang up in tree-shaded seclusion, terraces of town houses began to appear, and shops, hotels and churches added to the fabric of Ryde which became a borough in 1868. The extension of its pier and the coming of the railways, especially from Ryde pierhead to Ventnor, allowed a great increase in the amount of traffic between the town and Portsmouth.

Ryde has continued into the present as a fully-fledged town with a population of around 23,000. Its light industries and importance as a shopping centre maintain its life out of the tourist season and in spite of its lengthy and commercialised esplanade the atmosphere of Ryde is semi-formal. The guide book which states that 'no discriminating tourist will linger in Ryde' presents a grossly false impression of a town that has a high sense of civic pride as revealed in the Town Hall, Market House and Royal Victoria Arcade, all now restored. Ryde, in fact, is one of the many British towns noted for its Victorian buildings, particularly churches such as Sir Gilbert Scott's All Saints (1867) whose lofty spire dominates the skyline, and hotels of which Ryde Castle, Ryde Esplanade and the Royal Squadron are fine examples of nineteenth-century architecture. The recently-restored Brigstocke Terrace, however, with its splendid façade overlooking the sea, is witness to Ryde's early development as a resort, for with its stuccoed Regency houses, it was an attempt to emulate similar terraces in Brighton.

COWES AND THE SQUADRON

The small port of Cowes grew rapidly during the nineteenth century to achieve fame as an international yachting centre and the home of the most exclusive sailing club in the world. Yachting was not a new pastime: Charles II, when staying in the Channel Islands, sailed a small boat round the coasts for pleasure and the Royal Cork Yacht Club had been established as early as 1720. Yet yachting on the scale that developed at Cowes was a new phenomenon for the local advantages were many: it was relatively near London especially with the growth of the railways, it had sheltered waters with four daily tides and, most important, there were many boat-builders and ancillary craftsmen who were skilled in the construction and maintenance of small craft.

Yachting, it is said, was born from the competition which developed between the fast smuggling luggers and the equally swift revenue cutters both, as previously mentioned, being specialities of Cowes. During the eighteenth century, wagers were apparently made on the outcome of contests between these fishing or smuggling craft and the pilot cutters, but the first recorded contest was in 1788 which was a race around the island by cutters. In the early years of the nineteenth century wealthy and titled people began to use Cowes as a vacation centre, and, in 1811, the Duke of Gloucester, for his own amusement, placed bets on local boats in unofficial races. This became so popular that in 1813 a formal regatta was organised when boats were chartered for racing purposes but manned by professional seamen. It was not long before the gentlemen themselves joined in the races and began to commission yachts and other craft built specifically for pleasure. Yachting was put on an organised basis after June 1815 when 'a group of enthusiastic gentlemen' under the guidance of the Honourable Charles Pelham (later Lord Yarborough) met at The Thatched House Tavern in St James Street, London and formed The Yacht Club, with forty-two members. The qualifications for entry were simple: good social standing, an entrance fee and a yacht over a certain tonnage. Within two years the Prince Regent requested to join the Club, initiating its long line of royal patronage, and in 1820 when he became King George IV the Club was renamed The Royal Yacht Club. It adopted as its uniform 'a common blue jacket with white trousers' described as being 'far from unbecoming to such as are not too square in the stern'.

Yet the Club was founded for a serious objective as well as for pleasure. It possessed several craft fitted out as men-of-war including Lord Yarborough's *Falcon*, built on the lines of a twenty-gun corvette and fully armed with a cannon. It was run on regulations conforming to those of the Royal Navy and before leaving England all *Falcon* hands signed a paper setting forth the merits of a flogging, if necessary to preserve discipline. By the 1840s the total armament of the Club was four hundred guns, making it a powerful naval force, owned by the British aristocracy. If it had a sea captain, then this was Lord Yarborough who died in September 1846 on board his yacht *Kestrel* in Vigo, Spain. The *Falcon* had previously been sold as an opium carrier!

119

In 1833, which marked the accession of William IV, the Club was renamed The Royal Yacht Squadron of which the king was 'graciously pleased to consider himself the head'. In the same year Princess Victoria began to take an interest in its activities and her mother, the Duchess of Kent, presented the challenge cup. In 1838 Queen Victoria and Prince Albert became members and Tsar Nicholas of Russia was the first member of a foreign royal family to join when he owned a Cowes-built yacht, appropriately named *Queen Victoria*. Naturally, a club with such prestige and patronage evolved elaborate ritualistic customs and to break any, especially the complicated flag-etiquette, was social death. None but members and officers of the Royal Navy could land at the graduated stage in front of the Squadron clubhouse which occupied the site of Henry VIII's West Cowes fort. The clubhouse itself was entirely a male domain; ladies were restricted to the lawn behind and it was not until the 1920s that a ladies room was provided. They were then allowed to lunch and dine within the precincts but only on certain days and within certain hours.

In 1863 the Prince of Wales became a patron, and from 1882 its Commodore, for nineteen years. This was the heyday of rich men's yachting when the cream of English society descended on the town especially in August for Cowes Week. It became one of the main social functions of the aristocratic year, sandwiched between the end of the London season and the recuperative round of the European spas in autumn. The town, however, which had received its 'lighting, cleansing and otherwise improving' Act as early as 1816, was still rather bedraggled and apparently unconcerned by the rank and fashion that thronged its seafront. Yet reports of rents of £70 a week for a sitting room and two bedrooms during Cowes Week must have made some impact and the narrow, winding, almost Dickensian main, or High Street, leading down to the Parade came to specialise in quality shops, catering largely for the needs of the sailing fraternity. 'By Royal Appointment' and 'Purveyor to Her Majesty' were, and still are, common signs on shop frontages, offices and workshops.

The exclusive days of yachting were those up to 1914 and Cowes also became the home of the Royal London Yacht Club, the Royal Corinthian Yacht Club, the Cowes Corinthian Yacht Club and the Island Sailing Club, the latter's current membership exceeding 3,000. Yachting is now more democratic and clubhouses pepper the island's shore from Yarmouth to Bembridge. Cowes Week remains, however, a major sporting and social event and vessels of members of the still exclusive RYS are privileged to fly the St George's ensign. Thus, like British naval ships, they were, formerly at least, admitted into all foreign ports free of harbour dues, a custom dating back to the time of Lord Yarborough.

VENTNOR AND THE CURE

The Victorian popularity of Ventnor and its surroundings was founded on medical opinion rather than on boats and was related to a visit in 1830 by the famous physician Sir James Clark. In a popular medical treatise published in 1841 and entitled *The Sanative Influence of Climate on Disease* he stressed the health advantages of Ventnor's equable climate, citing in particular the Undercliff as being beneficial for pulmonary disorders. 'I have certainly seen nothing along the south coast of England', he stated, 'that will bear comparison with the Ventnor area' whose mildness was exemplified by the way geraniums, palms, myrtles, petunias and even figs survived the winter out of doors. In an age of romantic magniloquence it is easy to appreciate how Ventnor subsequently became known as England's Madeira, Positano or Sorrento.

When Clark visited the area Ventnor was merely a picturesque cove with an inn (The Crab and Lobster), a corn mill turned by a small stream which fell in a cascade to the beach and a few fishermen's (and undoubtedly smugglers') cottages. Within years this settlement in Bonchurch parish became a kind of non-religious Lourdes for, as many as could afford it, came to take its air and water. The extent of the initial influx can be gauged from Ventnor's population figures which increased from 350 in 1838 to over 5,000 in 1866. These early visitors built themselves villas where they seasoned each year, but the speculators were quick to move in to cater for the growing demand for accommodation. There was, in fact, a race to exploit Ventnor, though it developed more as a watering-place than as a seaside resort and its hotels, churches, marine villas, town hall, esplanade and gardens gave it a sophisticated mid-nineteenth century character, of which much remains today.

It is anomalous that a health spa catering for the infirm should have developed on such a difficult site. St Boniface Down, which provides the beneficial shelter and southerly aspect, rises steeply from the shore and this dictated the form the town would take. Ventnor was built (rather than planned) as a series of ledges extending up the Downs, linked by circuitous, often zigzag, streets and roads and in its upper part by flights of steep steps. Thus every villa and hotel gained an uninterrupted view of the sea with front doors and small gardens often level with neighbours' roofs. The impression, and hence the Sorrento comparison, is of a tiered town with walled roads rising precipitously in a situation where building land is at a premium.

In 1846 an Act was passed for the 'paving, lighting, watching, cleansing and otherwise improvement of Ventnor' which was administered by a Board of Commissioners elected annually. Though an excellent water supply was obtained from the springs in the Down, other sanitary services, due to site difficulties, were initially disregarded. The situation was improved by the Local Government Act of 1858, but communications still proved to be a major hindrance to development. It was easier to reach Ventnor by sea than across the island and steamers from Littlehampton brought passengers and cargoes to a wooden pier which replaced a spit promontory that had protected Ventnor Bay from easterly winds. The removal of this protective breakwater meant that wave assault was concentrated on the pier itself which subsequently collapsed. The old promontory was artificially restored and a new pier was constructed in the 1880s. Ventnor's accessibility was greatly improved with the arrival of the railway, though the line from Ryde Pier was forced to tunnel through the Downs from the vicinity of Wroxall Manor Farm and terminate at the entrance of a dry valley above the town.

Many famous and influential people patronised Ventnor including Karl Marx and the young Winston Churchill in 1878. Ten years earlier in neighbouring St Lawrence the National Hospital for Diseases of the Chest was founded by Dr Arthur Hassall, who had himself spent some time in Ventnor for health reasons. It was an impressive series of block buildings, all facing south, and with balconies and verandahs overlooking extensive gardens linked to the shore by a tunnel. There were large donations to the hospital and its gardens, and many of its trees were formally planted by royal visitors. Though patients came from all over Britain, more than half of its residents were from London and its suburbs. As medical opinion changed with the discovery and use of antibiotics the number of patients dwindled and the hospital was forced to close in 1964. Indecision over its subsequent use led to the building's deterioration and demolition. Today the 30-acre site is occupied by the Ventnor Botanic Garden where plants in profusion, many of them exotic, are fitting reminders to the old hospital's *raison d'être*.

Ventnor has been forced to make other changes and adaptations over the last fifty years, though fortunately seaside commercialisation tends to be confined to the beach and esplanade. Its hilly site, by sheer force of gravity, dictates that this is the town's focal point and with pier, busy beach, boating lake, flower beds, Winter Gardens, band concerts, souvenir shops, amusement parks and bingo there is little here to distinguish it from numerous other southern English resorts. Yet a short, but steep, climb up Shore Hill into Pier Street and then the upper layers of the town is really a journey into time. Solid stone buildings with sash windows, low-pitched grey slate roofs and double-tiered iron balconies—totally unplanned, yet aesthetically pleasing—collectively retain the Victorian atmosphere which made Ventnor famous.

The island's railways were an integral part of the Victorian process of development and although by mainland standards they came late there was, nonetheless, a period of railway mania with piecemeal, unco-ordinated growth and a duplication of lines and, at Newport, stations. Towards the end of the nineteenth century no less than six companies operated a plethora of lines, all built with an eye on profits and the resultant competition in terms of fares and advertising was intense.

The first railway ran from Newport to Cowes and was the outcome of protracted negotiations initiated by Newport Town Council on 7 November 1845. Largely because of the opposition from local landlords and their reluctance to sell land, the railway was not incorporated until 8 August 1859, and the first passenger trains operated on 16 June 1862. This $4\frac{1}{2}$-mile long railway was a modest venture. Running along the west bank of the Medina it had encountered few engineering difficulties and its initial rolling stock was purchased second-hand from the mainland. When it was opened the Southampton to Cowes steamer service was the main entry to the island and Cowes was also the main coal port. In 1870, and in conjunction with the railway. Medina Wharf was built upstream to handle coal and other bulky freight for Newport and other parts of the island.

The second railway venture was developed mainly to cater for, or attract, the tourist trade. This was the Isle of Wight Railway (IOWR) which was incorporated in July 1860, and linked Ryde with Ventnor via Brading, Sandown, Shanklin and Wroxall. The line reached Shanklin in 1862 and the company's original intention was to continue it southwards to Ventnor by way of Luccombe, the Landslip and Bonchurch.

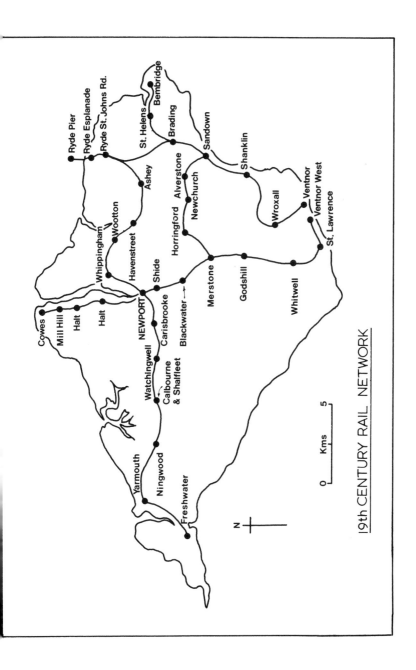

Ryde Pier
Ryde Esplanade
Ryde St. Johns Rd.
St. Helens
Bembridge
Brading
Sandown
Shanklin
Ventnor
Ventnor West
St. Lawrence
Wroxall
Ashey
Alverstone
Newchurch
Horringford
Wootton
Whippingham
Havenstreet
Shide
Merstone
Godshill
Whitwell
NEWPORT
Carisbrooke
Blackwater →
Watchingwell
Calbourne
& Shalfleet
Cowes
Mill Hill
Halt
Halt
Yarmouth
Ningwood
Freshwater

N

0   Kms   5

19th CENTURY RAIL NETWORK

Opposition, chiefly from Lord Yarborough, caused this scheme to be abandoned in favour of a route via Wroxall which necessitated an expensive 1,312yd long tunnel through St Boniface Down. In view of the many coastal landslides this proved to be a more sensible course and on 10 September 1866, the railway reached Ventnor, but terminated in a station inconveniently situated 294ft above sea level.

The success of the Cowes and Newport and the Isle of Wight Railways encouraged the promotion of other companies which were to prove less profitable. In 1880 Sandown was linked with Newport via a wide loop through Newchurch and Merstone and in the same year the line from Newport to Ryde via Whippingham, Wootton and Havenstreet was opened. Although initially independent these lines which focused on Newport were amalgamated in 1887 to form the Isle of Wight Central Railway (IOWCR). It also included a branch line from Brading to St Helens and Bembridge, but its most important development was the construction in 1880 of railway tracks along Ryde pier to connect boats with stations in the town and hence the island network.

In 1888–9 freight and passenger trains began running on the first and only railway to be built in West Wight. This was the Freshwater, Yarmouth and Newport Railway, but proposals to extend it to the fashionable and growing Totland Bay were vigorously opposed by the local farmers. The last section of the island's network was the short branch line from Merstone on the Sandown–Newport line, south through Godshill, Whitwell and St Lawrence to Ventnor. This was an attempt by the IOWCR, in conjunction with the Southampton, Isle of Wight and South of England Royal Mail Steam Packet Company Ltd (Red Funnel Steamers), to approach Ventnor via Cowes and break the monopoly of holiday traffic to that town held by the IOWR. The line, which opened on 26 July 1897, was under a nominally independent company and its terminus, later to be known as West Ventnor, was situated near the grounds of Steephill Castle, nearly a mile from the town centre.

Though improved communications greatly affected the

growth and style of Ventnor, Ryde and other coastal resorts, it was at Shanklin and, in particular, at Sandown, that the new character of tourism was reflected. As late as 1846 Lord Jeffrey wrote that Shanklin 'village is very small and scattery' and even by 1855 it was still a collection of thatched cottages (with some villa development) and, at the bottom of the chine, a few fishermen's houses. Three years after the arrival of the railway the esplanade was built and development along the front was rapid although, because of steep cliffs, it was only one row deep and in 1891 the first lift was constructed to connect the shore with the cliff-top development.

Sandown's growth was even later but, like Shanklin, its excellent beach and sheltered position with a high sunshine record, guaranteed it a future. From a 'mere village by a sandy shore', as Sandown had been described, it grew into the most unashamedly commercialised of all the Wight resorts. With little of architectural merit, its rapid growth was to link it, via Lake, with Shanklin, thus forming a continuous holiday strip extending for three miles around Sandown Bay. Today the town's esplanade is a mile of bars and cafes, a pier, amusement arcades, hotels and boarding houses, gardens, swimming pool and bingo halls. Behind is a prosperous town which is saved from becoming an Isle of Wight Blackpool by its library which houses the island's Geological Museum with a display of maps, rocks and fossils. Amongst its famous visitors were Charles Darwin who began his controversial *Origin of Species* when staying in Sandown, Sir Isaac Pitman who obviously found it more colourful and entertaining than his shorthand manual, and Lewis Carroll, who, today, in Sandown, would have been inspired for many a bizarre journey into wonderland.

Following the arrival of the railways the population of the Isle of Wight rapidly increased. From a figure of 22,000 in 1801 it grew to around 74,000 in 1881 and for the decade 1861–71 the annual rate was nearly a thousand a year, an increase never equalled since. This was obviously not the result of natural increase alone for, as previously stated, there were many, especially the leisured classes, who settled in the coastal towns to give them an air of fashionable prosperity. Many have claimed that the Victorian discovery and breakdown of isolation spoiled the Isle of Wight. Certainly it led to administrative uniformity and to a modifying of traditions, but the personalities it produced and the townscapes it provided must be seen to compensate for any dilution of the island's local peculiarities.

9   THE ISLAND ECONOMY

To the garden isle came the tourist trade,
The Needles an afternoon trip,
'Five bob all around the Island',
In a snorting little ship.

Leslie Thomas

THE Solent which has given the Isle of Wight so much of its character, dictated most of its history, and acted as the chief preserver of its individualism, is today a major stumbling block to the island's economy. Not to tourism, for insularity, as in Victorian and Edwardian times, proves a great attraction to pleasure seekers, but to other branches of the economy the island's geographical situation presents major problems in the form of higher transport costs and charges. From the bulk freight quays at Cowes, East Cowes, Newport, and to a limited extent Yarmouth and Bembridge, the higher Solent transfer costs are twofold: the charges of goods and services imported from the mainland are inflated, and the commodities produced locally and exported are often placed at a competitive disadvantage with mainland goods. The movement of manufactured goods and of agricultural and horticultural produce are both affected and the change from one mode of transport to another, with inevitable delays, sometimes lengthy in inclement weather, aggravates the situation.

In addition to the cost of insularity (yet partly the result of it) most branches of the island's economy suffered a severe downward trend after 1958. Changes in central government defence policy resulted in the rundown of the two major employing industries — shipbuilding and aircraft manufacturing — which caused approximately 2,000 redundancies. Important changes in agriculture also meant the loss of a work force of about 1,000 and the numbers employed in the construction industry declined by a quarter. Although by present standards the island's unemployment figure of 4 per cent seems low, it meant that the island's towns were listed as Development Areas under the Local Employment Act of 1960. Financial incentive and local council initiative did much to attract several new and diversified industries for land values were attractive, wage rates were lower, house prices cheaper and a pool of surplus labour was readily available. Thus, today the island's economic base is more diverse and better spread over manufacturing, agriculture, tourism and services but again there are signs of a downward trend. Problems accrue from inequalities in job structure, population imbalance with a shortage of people of working age for 'key' jobs, and unemployment. Except during the comparatively short summer season, the unemployment is considerably above both the south-east region and the national level. In 1975–6, winter unemployment reached almost 10 per cent and for 1976–7 it was 9 per cent. Thus tourism is not the panacea for the island's economic problems, though obviously, together with its supportive trades and services, it is one on which the Isle of Wight places great dependence. One of the main policy targets of the county council is to secure industries which will counter the serious seasonal and general unemployment figures. In January 1977 the latter was 3,141 or 8.3 per cent of its active working force, 2·7 per cent higher than the national average. Of those unemployed, 45 per cent were under thirty years of age, a factor which can obviously be related to corresponding migration statistics.

The island's number of registered employees is in the region of 38,000 of which some 14,000 are females. An analysis of the 1975 statistics for the local labour exchanges (see table)

Employment by local exchanges (1975), totals and percentages

	Newport		Cowes		Ryde		Sandown		Ventnor		Freshwater	
Primary	649	5·1	41	0·5	64	0·9	173	2·7	144	6·4	68	3·4
Manufacturing	2014	15·8	5061	66·2	1152	16·8	871	13·4	244	10·8	447	22·3
Construction	441	3·5	67	0·9	487	7·1	624	9·6	136	6·0	165	8·2
Gas, Elect., Water	71	0·6	116	1·5	321	4·7	40	0·6	0	0	4	0·2
Distribution	1834	14·4	499	6·5	1098	16·0	797	12·2	268	11·9	242	12·1
Misc. Services	1695	13·3	589	7·7	1448	21·1	2520	38·7	824	36·6	711	35·5
Public Admin.	2193	17·2	297	3·9	321	4·7	124	1·9	218	9·7	53	2·1
Other Services	3819	30·0	976	12·8	1975	28·7	1361	20·9	418	18·6	323	16·1
Totals	12716	100%	7646	100%	6874	100%	6510	100%	2252	100%	2003	100%

Source: *Employment Records II* (*Census*)

illustrates the dominance of Cowes as the island's major manufacturing centre where two-thirds of its employees were in various industries. The table also emphasises Newport's role as the island's administrative and servicing centre whereas the coastal and rural areas of Freshwater, Ryde, Sandown and Ventnor were dominated by the tourist industry and it is in these areas that many of the island's economic and social problems are most acute. Agriculture and other primary occupations are poorly represented in all areas, but the inflated position of Newport in the primary sector is a reflection of its traditional position as the island's market town, and the general role of agriculture should not be underestimated.

AGRICULTURE

Although not a major direct employer of labour, agriculture is of vital importance to the economy of the Isle of Wight and to its rural scene in general. Over 75 per cent of the island is under agricultural management with a further 13 per cent of its area in non-urban use (forests, woodlands, nature reserves, etc.). In 1975 the number of persons working in agriculture (farmers, labourers and managers) was 1,650 (or 3 per cent of the total active labour force) of which around 700 were full-time regular, or hired workers. Within the last twenty years or so the number of workers employed on farms and other agricultural holdings has dramatically fallen, reflecting the general national picture. Mechanisation and better farm management is largely responsible for this, but the decline has recently slowed down or even levelled off as a result of developments in profitable labour intensive pursuits, particularly market gardening and horticulture. Studies have shown that in these sectors, glasshouses can support up to seven workers per acre for flowers, and slightly less for food crops, a figure considerably higher than that for other branches of farming. At harvest time the addition of casual labour will inflate this figure.

The island's low totals for those employed in agriculture should not disguise its general significance. A large number of ancillary and supportive trades, industries and professions are dependent on it and are associated in some way with the processing and selling of farm produce, or the servicing and maintenance of machinery, equipment and livestock. Haulage contractors, machinery agents, creamery and abattoir workers, together with many professionals such as auctioneers and valuers, estate agents and veterinary surgeons, all look to agriculture for their livelihood. Added to these of course are agricultural building specialists, glasshouse erectors and feed-mixing contractors.

In addition to the general reduction of farm workers, other island farming trends mirror similar changes on the mainland, especially in Hampshire and its neighbouring counties. Fluctuations in the arable acreage, the tendency towards barley cultivation, the rapid increase of dairying, the change to the cultivation of grasses and feed crops and the growing importance of horticulture have combined to change Wight farming from a mere livelihood into a profitable business run on lines similar to manufacturing industry. This is reflected both in the increased size of fields to facilitate further mechanisation and in the amalgamation of farms to produce more economic units and enterprises. The average farm size in 1968 was 76 acres which was slightly less than the national average of 83 acres. By 1972, however, the average farm size had risen to 90 acres and the trend continues. According to a recent report the number of agricultural holdings on the island has been reduced by a third since 1949, while the number of holdings above 300 acres have increased by over 50 per cent. On account of its physical diversity and the corresponding variation in soil types, the island produces a wide range of agricultural products which again qualifies it for the designation a 'miniature England'. However, a fundamental distinction in farming practice occurs between the northern Tertiary 'lowlands' whose generally ill-drained brown earths and gleys together with patches of acid and coarser textured podsolic soils support a predominantly dairying industry, and the remainder of the island where loams, sandy and chalk-derived soils support a greater variety of enterprises. The soils on parts of the central chalk ridge, as already inferred, support the close turf characteristic of downland which is important as summer grazing areas for sheep, though they share these pastures with cattle. The Greensand areas to the south also provide excellent pastureland as do the Wealden Beds to the east and west, and all contrast with the southern uplands and especially its margins, whose soils provide good arable tracts with large fields and some downland pasture. In general terms, dairying, livestock and horticulture are practised on smaller farms and holdings and arable farming on the larger units, especially in the centre of the island where fields are correspondingly large.

Dairying and Cereals

Milk production and cereals are the basis on which the island's farming economy turns and of the 67,000 acres in production, some 36,000 are under grass (temporary and permanent), 23,500 acres under some form of tillage (with 19,500 acres given to cereals) and the remainder is rough grazing. Of the cereals 15,000 acres are devoted to barley and 7,500 to wheat. Some 60 per cent of the island's full-time holdings, however, derive most of their income from milk production and although the advent of bulk milk collection has led to a dramatic fall in the number of registered dairy producers, the total island herd has tended to remain constant at around 11,500 animals. The production of milk has been increasing and the island exports dairy produce and liquid milk to the mainland.

Other Livestock

The number of pigs, an enterprise traditionally associated with dairying, gravitates around the 17,000 figure and most of the production is for pork, though some bacon pigs go to the mainland. The Isle of Wight pigs, like the Hampshire Hogs, are noted for their good quality pork, and its beef herd of around 3,000 head is of equally good quality. The number of sheep, the traditional livestock of the downlands, have fluctuated depending on the economic climate for mutton, wool or grains, but currently their numbers are again on the increase with a total of around 10,000. The flocks are chiefly associated with the central ridge. Chickens and other birds are, of course, ubiquitous and collectively they number at least 75,000.

Horticulture

This farming enterprise now plays an increasingly important part in the island's agricultural and general economy, both in the production of outdoor vegetables and in the modern glasshouse sector. It is an industry well attuned to the tourist trade, with the production of fresh fruit and vegetables reaching a peak when the island's population expands to its highest numbers in the summer months.

Private investment and grant aids to horticulture have been considerable, and the island can now compete fairly successfully with comparable areas on the mainland. Long sunshine hours, particularly in winter, and an extended growing season, combine with markets to make the Isle of Wight one of the most rapidly developing horticultural areas in Britain. The industry is concentrated mainly in the Arreton valley where well-drained and fertile soils, level land, an adequate water supply and shelter from winds provide most suitable requirements for glasshouse and open horticultural development. Other parts of the island specialising in horticulture include the St Lawrence, Chale and Brook areas along the south coast and the Wootton area in the north-east.

Of the 40 acres (1976) or so under glass, about half is devoted to tomato production, with a large percentage of the produce finding ready markets on the mainland. The amount of vegetables, excluding potatoes, grown in the open has also increased over the last few years and in 1976 covered 1,000 acres. Wight potatoes, in fact, are amongst the earliest in the country with around 400 acres given to 'earlies' and 900 acres to the main crop. Sweet corn, cucumbers, cabbages, sprouts, cauliflowers, peas and carrots are also grown for local and mainland markets and there has been a steady expansion in the fresh flower trade.

In 1967 7½ acres at Arreton were devoted to carnations, a labour-intensive crop (on account of the need for constant disbudding to achieve a good single bloom) using local female labour. The success of this venture led to the cultivation of early chrysanthemums and roses which find out-of-season markets throughout the British Isles.

The economic advantages of horticulture, especially where glasshouses reduce the growing time of plants, means that two crops can often be obtained in a year. Insularity, however, is a major problem in the competition for mainland markets and one method in use at present to accelerate despatch is bulk transport where, as with milk, produce is loaded into large lorries or containers and is transported cheaper than would otherwise be possible.

Fruit Crops

Orchards have never been commercially important in the Isle of Wight for the south-westerly salt-laden winds are a severe limiting factor for top fruit growing. The island has a modest acreage under small fruits, however, where strawberries tend to be the main crop, and in an attempt to emulate earlier experiments there are vineyards at Adgestone and Cranmore, near Brading. Here the sunshine record is equal to, if not higher than, many of the German vine-growing districts, though temperatures are not as warm. The well-tended vineyards enjoy good harvests and the Adgestone Dry White Wine is a successful vintage, supplying a London distributor as well as a growing local demand in hotels throughout the island.

OTHER PRIMARY INDUSTRIES

The character and extent of the island's forests and woodlands, natural and planted, has already been discussed in an earlier chapter. It was noted that around 9 per cent of the island has a forest cover of which some 60 per cent is managed by the

Forestry Commission. The small-scale felling of hardwoods and conifers every four or five years, together with thinning programmes, gives a total timber yield of some 2,500 tons per annum. Most is shipped to the mainland for use as wood pulp, wood wool, logs and stakes. Although they add considerably to the island's scenic attractiveness, forests and woodlands are not great employers of labour and only a small number of foresters and contractors are needed to manage them efficiently.

There are also very few people actively engaged in the island's fisheries, though no figures are available for those in part-time employment. Oysters, crabs, lobsters and other shellfish are landed at various harbours and their main markets are the local hotels and restaurants, especially in the tourist season, though some reach mainland fish markets. Newtown estuary is the traditional home of the island's oysters which have been gathered here, probably since Roman times. By the 1950s, however, the industry had run down and an attempt to revive it proved unsuccessful. Small oysters from France were introduced, especially to the section of the estuary known as Clamerkin Lake, but they almost all perished in the Arctic winter of 1962, including the oysters in other parts of The Solent area. By sheer fluke of circumstances American clams were flourishing in Southampton Water and were introduced to the Newtown River where they thrived and gradually won markets in France, chiefly Brittany, and in London. By 1977 the oyster survivors had re-colonised the Solent mudflats, including the Newtown estuary. Over the past four years the island's catch has averaged around £38,000 for shellfish (including crabs and lobsters) and just under £3,000 for plaice, cod, sole and other wet fish.

Limestone, chalk, sand, gravel and clay are the only minerals worked on the island and the labour force is small (0.2% of active employment). Their extraction is mainly to meet the demands of the local construction trade.

MANUFACTURING INDUSTRY

As previously mentioned, the decline in shipbuilding, marine engineering and other key employment industries resulted in a powerful drive in the late 1950s and '60s to attract light industrial enterprises. These were seen as a balance to decline and as a buffer to further fluctuations. As a result, the island now has a wide range of modern and expanding industries though its main manufacturing pivots are still those traditionally associated with the island such as the plants and firms of Cowes harbour which, not surprisingly, still have close affinities with the sea.

Earlier chapters have discussed the boat-building activities of Cowes with reference to ships for the Royal Navy, fast smuggling vessels and equally fast pilot and customs cutters. By 1846 John and Robert White, in conjunction with their neighbour, Andrew Lamb, became important manufacturers of lifeboats for stations around Britain, and Lamb and White boats gained certificates from the Royal National Lifeboat Institution. These boats were designed on whaler lines and around 130 wooden lifeboats were constructed. Torpedo boats and destroyers, it appears, evolved from this design, again with important Admiralty orders. HMS *Crusader* of World War I was involved in reconnoitring work off the Ostend coast and is one of Lamb and White's most famous boats, as is the *Mohawk* which, after being blown open by a mine, was structurally sound enough to be towed home. Between the wars the yard produced a variety of craft ranging from paddle steamers to the chain ferry across the Medina, but its last naval frigate was the *Arethusa* and subsequently it specialised in large yachts and cargo boats. The yard's boat-building activities were terminated in 1965 with a consequent reduction of its workforce from 2,500 to 400, yet it maintained something of its maritime tradition by manufacturing bow thrusters for tankers and special hoists for bringing pilots aboard. It remains one of many industries in Cowes with similar connections, for there are a number of yacht and boat-builders with supportive trades that specialise in sails, nautical instruments, ship-rigging and allied maritime crafts.

East Cowes in particular is a jumble of manufacturing premises and offices of which its biggest industry, with a workforce of 2,000, is the British Hovercraft Corporation. This covers a site of 60 acres flanking the Medina River with other sites near Osborne House which are its technical, design and electronic centres. The firm's origins can be traced to Moses Saunders who, in 1834, set up a boat-building business at Streatly-on-Thames. This proved so successful that in 1901 his grandson transferred the business to East Cowes in order to have better access to water. High speed boats were its speciality and, after 1945, drawing on wartime experience of building amphibious vessels, the firm produced the world's largest flying boats, the Princesses. These proved to be commercial flops, but in 1959, after much experimentation, the first air-cushioned vehicle, the SR NI Hovercraft, appeared, from which a number of types and sizes developed. Hovercrafts have since proved indispensable throughout the world on expeditions, to armies, and in more conventional communications, for example, between the island and the mainland.

Another of the island's notable industries is that of Britten & Norman, located at Bembridge Airport, specialising in small aircraft. Initially the firm bought surplus trainer aircraft and converted them for such uses as crop-spraying, but in 1963 the first Islander was planned and it appeared in 1967. Orders increased and after the firm joined Fairey Aviation in 1972 a new production line was set up in Belgium. Britten & Norman specialise in orders for flying ambulances, businessmen's aircraft, planes for air photography and for pest control. The success of the two engine plane led to the bigger 17-seater, Trislander, and the Defender, a military version of the Islander which is in service in Jamaica, Hong Kong and Guyana. The Ski-Islander is a new amphibious Islander.

Yachts, hovercrafts and small planes have earned national and internatinal reputations for Isle of Wight industry as has Plesseys of Someton which manufacture advanced electronic systems and radar equipment. These, however, are just part, albeit an important one, of a very broad range of manufacturing industries. Cowes is undoubtedly the island's manufacturing centre but Newport and Ryde have a number of firms, and other establishments are located throughout the island. As far as rural industry is concerned the island authorities enjoy a close working relationship with CoSIRA (Council for Small Industries in Rural Areas) and since 1972 have distributed some £400,000 in loans to thirty island firms. Among its schemes is the establishment of a small industrial estate at Ventnor whose products include glass fibre boats, plastic mouldings and Venetian blinds, and the development of six 'nursery' units at Newport Industrial Estate, the aim being to provide suitable accommodation for small industries to establish themselves in the hope that they will expand.

The island naturally has industries which stem from the needs of tourism and one which has a national reputation is J. Arthur Dixon Ltd which manufactures greetings cards and stationery. Jewellery, novelties, confectionery, souvenir dolls, hand-made glass, pottery and ceramics are aimed at both local and wider tourist markets.

TOURISM

The beginnings of this industry have been discussed in earlier chapters and throughout this century, especially since World War II, the importance of the island as a tourist centre has rapidly increased. Its popularity has been sustained by its climate, which is good by British standards, its scenic attractions in an insular setting, and its ready access to London and the Midlands. As an economic provider tourism has its disadvantages for the island season is comparatively short and in common with other national resorts it has to contend with the fierce competition of continental holidays.

In spite of its size and of this competition the island caters for a surprisingly large number of visitors and a high proportion of what is described in tourist terms as 'holiday weeks'. In June,

July and August, the high season months, both the ferries and the island's available accommodation are used to capacity. In 1974, for example, the island catered for 1·10 million holiday weeks and there were 6,555,580 total travellers on all ferry routes, a figure which did not include those who arrived in private boats or who used the airport at Bembridge. Thus it appears that on average the population of the island is something like 140,000 (ranging from say 115,000 to almost 200,000 depending on months), rather than the 110,000 resident level which is normally quoted in statistics. This is reflected in the increase in the number of cars which in 1974 inflated the residential registered motor vehicles in one peak week from 41,000 to 57,000.

Although no official survey has been made concerning the origins of visitors to the Isle of Wight, a sample survey was carried out by a German research student at Sandown in July 1968 and July 1970. Based on some 500 sample interviews it indicated that the London area, the West Midlands, Manchester, Liverpool and Lancashire generally, and West Yorkshire were the chief tourist reservoirs, at least for the popular beach-type holiday which Sandown provides. Wales and the south-west peninsula, in spite of their good communications with Southampton, provided few tourists as did East Anglia, northern England, Scotland and Ireland.

Part of the Isle of Wight's tourist appeal is its ability to offer a wide range of different types of holidays and facilities. These range from the Ryde, Shanklin and Sandown seaside town holidays where the visitor is one of a crowd, to organised holiday camps, camping holidays, sailing holidays or just quiet holidays. The demand for the latter is increasing rapidly so protection and preservation of natural amenities is uppermost in planners' minds in order to retain some sort of balance.

10   ISLAND LIFE AND PROBLEMS

*In no way can it be said on the basis of . . . .
socio-economic evidence that the Island acts
in relation to Portsmouth as part of its city
region.*

Isle of Wight County Council Report, 1969

LOCAL GOVERNMENT

I N 1969 the Isle of Wight County Council presented a report
to the Royal Commission on Local Government in England
and Wales which was a fiercely argued attack against
proposals for incorporating the island into Hampshire for local
government purposes. The administrative viability of the
island was in question as was its degree of dependence on the
mainland and the character of trans-Solent business, social
and other contacts.

This was not the first time that the administrative
independence of the island had figured prominently in regional
and national politics. In 1880, with the passing of the Local
Government Act, which effectively established Britain's local
county system, the Isle of Wight formed part of the
administrative county of Hampshire, featuring rather
diminutively in documents, reports and laws. Although, by the
end of the nineteenth century, it was not impracticable for
island representatives to travel to Winchester a case was made
for its own separation and on 1 April 1890 the Isle of Wight
became a separate administrative county. Newport, for both
historical and practical reasons, became the seat of its county

council, functioning at a level higher than the local boroughs, urban and rural districts.

In 1972, however, the administrative independence of the island was challenged for the Local Government Act proposed its amalgamation with Hampshire. This was fiercely fought and a successful publicity campaign, arguing once again the difficulties involved in sending representatives to Winchester, won the island's case. There was some reorganisation, however, for the old local councils were amalgamated into two new districts. The Boroughs of Newport and Ryde, together with Cowes Urban District, formed the Borough of Medina and the Sandown and Shanklin and the Ventnor Urban District Councils merged with the Isle of Wight Rural District Council to form the Borough of South Wight. Close liaison and co-operation exists between these authorities and the County Council, and there are many common committees such as the Planning Management Committee for the whole island. These preclude any duplication between the authorities and provide a major saving on the rates bill.

Local government status has greatly added to the importance of Newport whose activities today, as in the past, are purely businesslike and functional and are not geared to the attraction of tourists (though it houses the offices of the Isle of Wight Tourist Board). Its largest and most impressive modern building is the County Council Offices in Lower High Street.

The Governor

In 1888 Queen Victoria revived the practice of the fourteenth and fifteenth centuries by granting the Governorship to a member of the royal family. Between 1889 and 1896 it was Prince Henry Maurice of Battenberg, husband of Victoria's youngest daughter, Princess Beatrice. The Prince died of fever in 1896 while serving in the Ashanti Expeditionary Force and Princess Beatrice succeeded him and retained the Governorship until her own death in 1944. The office remained in the Crown until 1957 when Gerald Wellesley, 7th Duke of Wellington, was appointed. On his resignation, Admiral of the

Fleet, the Earl Mountbatten of Burma, received the Letters Patent of Appointment on 19 July 1965. In 1972 he also became the island's first Lord-Lieutenant.

The modern office of Governor is purely an honorary title and there is no involvement in the administration of the county. The islanders, however, are proud of its tradition and having their own representative of the Crown adds to their sense of distinctiveness.

POPULATION

The island's greatest population increases were in Victorian times when the number of its inhabitants increased from 24,102 in 1812 to 73,044 in 1882. Since this time it has increased by about 50 per cent and after remaining fairly static after World War II, reached a figure of 110,900 in 1974. This was broken down as 65,100 for Medina Borough and 45,800 for South Wight Borough. Such a sub-division is not, however, of great significance for in reality it is the entire east and centre of the island which contains the greatest proportion, where 75 per cent live in the towns, all being coastal, except for Newport. Newport and Ryde challenge each other as being the island's largest centres in terms of population size and hover around the 22,000 mark. They are followed by Cowes, the island's major centre for production, with 19,000. Shanklin and Sandown are less than half this size, but collectively, and with the inclusion of Lake, they comprise a continuous settlement of around 18,000, three times the size of Ventnor.

The island's population growth and structure, however, reveal some interesting and unusual trends for natural increase has shown a continued decline since 1950 which means that the increases of around 1,000 persons per annum are due solely to migration. Here the structure of its population is significant for the non-productive sections of the community, namely the retired element, are increasing substantially as a proportion of the total, and the working population shows a considerable decline. Areas of the island which have a significant under-representation of working age groups, and hence a high retiral population, are West Wight (Totland, Freshwater, etc.) and the east and south-east coastal areas. Though Cowes and Newport have higher proportions of potentially economically active persons, they too fall below the national average. In 1971 the national average of retired persons (males over sixty-five years and females over sixty years) as a percentage of the total population was 15·6 per cent, while the Isle of Wight average was 24·8 and in a number of areas, especially the Ventnor–St Lawrence districts, was in excess of 30 per cent, double the national figure. Such trends influence not just industry but also the health and education systems and the housing and property markets.

Migration

In a recent report submitted by the County Council to the Development Commission it was noted that in the five years immediately preceding the 1971 Census a total of 21,030 persons moved into the island (19,320 from the rest of Britain and 1,710 from other countries). For the same period a total of 9,250 persons moved from the Isle of Wight to various mainland destinations. The report's analysis of these figures showed clearly that it was the young working population that was leaving the island, to be replaced by persons nearing or of pensionable age. Of those leaving the island 30·5 per cent were aged between 20 and 29 years, while 28·1 per cent of the immigrants were aged 60 and over.

Commuting

In view of the short distances involved and the good road and bus service, commuting within the island presents few serious problems. Of more interest are the number of islanders who travel to work on the mainland of which the chief groups seem to be engineers, boat-builders, construction workers, electricians, office workers and teachers who work in Southampton, Portsmouth and Lymington. Higher travel costs and longer journey times naturally characterise this trans-Solent commuting, but the frequent and efficient vessels that ply the channel make it feasible. This is, of course, a two-way movement but whereas an estimated 700 or so work on the mainland, only about 200 travel to the island for employment.

COMMUNICATIONS

From the intricate pattern, especially in east Wight, the island's railway network with its thirty-five stations and halts has been eroded to one last line that connects Ryde Pier Head (and hence by ferry to Portsmouth Harbour) with Ryde Esplanade, Ryde St John's Road, Brading, Sandown and Shanklin. Road competition, convenient bus services, the advent of cheaper motoring and Beeching's axe collectively brought about the downfall of a system which will long be mourned by railway enthusiasts, not to mention the inhabitants of Ventnor, when frosty conditions can prevent its access by road. This occurred in the long and severe winter of 1962–3 and the only public transport out of the town was the train to Shanklin and Ryde. This section of the line was closed in 1966, exactly one hundred years after its opening. In the same year the lines from Newport to Cowes and Newport to Ryde were also considered obsolete but the island's other lines had closed before this date. The Newport to Ventnor line closed down in 1952, the Bembridge to Brading and the Newport to Freshwater in 1953 and the line from Newport to Sandown, via Merstone, in 1956.

The 8·4 miles of track from Ryde Pier Head to Shanklin is obviously kept alive by the summer tourist influx and it is an electrified line on the third-rail system, as is the standard for the Southern Region. The old steam coaching stock were replaced by ex-London Transport underground trains (from the Piccadilly Line) and these now provide one service an hour in each direction and one train every two hours on Sundays. At the height of the tourist season, particularly on Saturdays, the service is increased.

Wight must be one of the few places in the British Isles where its surviving train service ignores the capital town. Newport, however, is the pivot of the island's road network and the headquarters of the Southern Vectis Omnibus Company whose buses meet ferries and link the town with every other town, village and hamlet. The system is a little more complex than this for villages are linked with the towns nearest them and the towns themselves have efficient and frequent connections. Regular services are increased and lengthened in summer (making changes unnecessary) and late buses tend to leave after the close of cinemas, concerts and other forms of entertainment.

The island has no motorways, nor long stretches of dual carriageways, and its roads vary from the standard 'A' road to narrow, winding country roads and lanes. Collectively there are over 450 miles of well-maintained roads but these are more often subject to acute, sharp bends than on the mainland and gradients are particularly steep, especially in the Ventnor area.

The ferry and other connections with the mainland have already been discussed and, weather permitting, the various forms of sea transport keep to an accurate timetable. Even during 'Cowes Week' the ferries, hydrofoils and hovercrafts manage to maintain a regular service in the midst of sails, sheets and spinnakers. Slight delays, as a result of passing boats, however, are often caused on the short chain-ferry crossing between East and West Cowes, a journey which otherwise necessitates a road detour via Newport. At Cowes there are on average some 7,000 ferry crossings a year, 9,500 hovercraft, 7,900 hydrofoil, 1,200 tankers, cargo ships and coasters, together with an incalculable number of yachting movements.

HOUSING AND COST OF LIVING

Prior to the boom in private housing in the late 1960s and early 1970s residential land values and property prices were well below those of the mainland, at least those of the south-east region. Both local residents and immigrant workers could usually afford to take out mortgages and enter the private property market. In recent years, however, the gap between the island and mainland property markets has rapidly narrowed, especially as prices are now inflated by the high demand for retiral homes. Naturally, it is the island's coasts and its most scenic parts which are the most expensive areas of the property market and the retired groups, having ready cash from the sale of other homes or businesses, are freed from mortgage liabilities. This greatly affects the position of local home ownership creating, in turn, an increased demand for rented accommodation which is in shorter supply. The sub-division of large houses to provide self-catering holiday flats and the rapid spread of 'second homes' greatly aggravates the position.

Though a large proportion of island homes are today owner-occupied, the two borough councils are responsible for local authority housing—its construction, improvement grant schemes, and the clearance of dilapidated dwellings. The housing waiting lists for the Medina Borough Council are 1,760 and for South Wight Borough Council 850. Their combined house building programmes for 1975–6 were 290 residences and for 1976–7, 380 residences. The island has two registered Housing Associations: one based on the local churches is concerned to meet accommodation shortages on humanitarian grounds; the other is backed by the Isle of Wight Chamber of Commerce, which recognises housing as an important factor in attracting workers to expanding or new industries and in retaining the island's population. Established in 1974, the Vectis Housing Association's main objective has been the provision of rented homes for persons whom they term the 'key workers' in industry and manufacturing.

If some house prices are still marginally lower than those of the mainland, any advantages accruing from this are lost by the general higher costs and prices for food and goods—the inevitable effect of insularity. As long ago as 1962 the County Council, in a bid for increased government aid, submitted evidence that island prices were some 4·5 per cent above those on the mainland. For most commodities this excess must inevitably be greatly increased in 1978. The Isle of Wight Consumer Group is studying the existing differential between island and mainland.

SHOPPING FACILITIES

The island has five shopping centres ranging from Newport and Ryde, which compete for the largest retail turnover, to the small centre at Ventnor. Sandown and Shanklin are the other towns with a shopping hinterland, though they have a large proportion of small novelty and gift shops, etc. which are dependent on the summer season trading.

Due to the limited size of the island's population and hence its limited turnover, it has not attracted the large national department stores and whereas Woolworth has a number of branches, there is no Marks and Spencer or British Home Stores. These stores normally demand at least a guaranteed catchment area of 100,000 inhabitants. The island's population has now reached this figure and is boosted far above it in summer. It is reasonable to assume, therefore, that the opening of such a store, centrally situated at Newport, would discourage shoppers from making trips to the mainland. An early study in 1966, carried out by the Isle of Wight Consumer Group, showed that 7 per cent of its population visited the mainland for shopping trips at least once a month and 40 per cent at least every three months. They also found that over 50 per cent of the purchases made on the mainland were of clothing. The great magnet was Marks and Spencer and the island is almost equally divided, in terms of retail attractiveness, between the areas of Southampton and Portsmouth.

The Isle of Wight, however, is not really a part of the 'city regions' of either of these mainland centres, though obviously proximity does exert some important influences. In newspapers, for example, the island's mainland affinities are expressed by the popularity of the *Evening News* (Portsmouth) and the *Southampton Evening Echo* (Southampton and Newport),

149

the former playing a particularly prominent role in those areas of the island adjacent to and served by Ryde Pier. The island's local newspapers are the *Isle of Wight County Press*, a voluminous paper of large format published at Newport on Saturdays and the Portsmouth-printed *Isle of Wight Weekly Post* of similar local interest. The district papers are Sandown and Shanklin's *Chronicle and Guardian* (published Thursdays), Ryde's *Times* (Thursdays) and Ventnor's *Mercury*.

SPORT AND ENTERTAINMENT

The island naturally has a wide range of outdoor pursuits for people of all financial classes and inclinations. Yachting and sailing is now a much more democratic pastime and local clubs and mooring facilities are found throughout the island with every requirement for the professional and amateur sailor. Other water sports include water-skiing, bathing on the island's innumerable and sometimes (still) uncrowded beaches, and sea fishing, which on the northern coast is characterised by flounder, mullet, plaice, bass and conger and in the Ventnor area by pollock, mullet, skate and bass. Sole, conger, bass and dogfish may be caught between Brook and Freshwater Bay. There is some fresh-water fishing at venues such as Gunville Lake, Somerton Reservoirs and sections of the East Yar.

Island cinemas have vanished from all but the main towns and holiday centres. Ryde has its triple auditorium complex, Newport has two cinemas, one twinning with a bingo hall, and Sandown, Shanklin and Ventnor each have one cinema. They all belong to the Star Entertainment circuit which show current films, but change their programmes frequently in a rotating pattern between eight halls. During the tourist season 'summer spectaculars' are presented at the pier complexes of the main resorts and both popular comedies and drama are presented at the Shanklin Theatre. Numerous clubs, public houses and restaurants throughout the island provide cabaret and entertainment.

Pub life is as active as in any part of England and the island has many historically interesting hostelries such as The Castle and The Bugle in Newport with their Charles I connections or another Bugle in Yarmouth which is one of the island's original coaching inns. The Buddle at Niton with its smuggling associations has already been referred to. The majority of inns and public houses are now part of national chains, but the island still has its century-old brewery at Ventnor which sells its beer chiefly in the town but also in inns at Shanklin, Freshwater, Wroxall and Arreton where in the latter, the Hare and Hounds provides a spectacular view over the island. The Newport pubs are particularly interesting on market days when there are extended licences, but at all times they are the island's main meeting places, preserving much of the local tradition, even if today this is slightly sacrificed to the now ubiquitous darts craze.

BIBLIOGRAPHY

BARLEY, M. W. (ed)., *The Plans and Topography of Medieval Towns in England and Wales*, Research Report No 14, The Council for British Archaeology, 1976

BERESFORD, M. W., *New Towns of the Middle Ages*, Lutterworth Press, 1967

BOWEN, M., *The Scandal of Sophie Dawes*, John Lane, 1935

BOWLE, J., *Charles the First*, Weidenfeld & Nicolson, 1975

CHARLTON, J., *Osborne House*, HMSO, 1977

DARBY, H. C. and CAMPBELL, E. M. J., *The Domesday Geography of South-East England*, Cambridge University Press, 1962

DOWLING, R. F. W., *Smuggling on Wight Island*, Clarendon Press (Ventnor), 1978

DYER, J., *Southern England: An Archaeological Guide*, Faber & Faber, 1977

GIROUARD, M., *The Victorian County House*, Clarendon Press (Oxford), 1971

HILLIER, GEORGE, *A Narrative of the attempted escapes of Charles the First from Carisbrooke Castle*, London, 1853

HUGHES, P., *The Isle of Wight*, Faber & Faber, 1967

Isle of Wight County Council, *County Structure Plan*, 1976

JONES, B., *The Isle of Wight*, Penguin Books, 1950

KOKERITZ, H., *The Place-names of the Isle of Wight*, Uppsala, 1940

LEWIS, M., *Spithead, An Informal History*, Allen & Unwin, 1972

LONG, W. H. (ed), *Dictionary of the Isle of Wight Dialect*, London, 1886

—— *The Oglander Memoirs*, London, 1888

LYON, B., *The Isle of Wight Companion*, Isle of Wight County Press, 1977

MCINNES, R., *Isle of Wight*, Collins, 1974

MONKHOUSE, F. J., *A Survey of Southampton and its Region*, British Association, 1964

National Trust, *Newtown, Isle of Wight and Bembridge Windmill* (nd)

NOYES, H., *The Isle of Wight Bedside Anthology*, Isle of Wight County Press, 1973

OGLANDER, C. ASPINALL, *Nunwell Symphony*, Hogarth Press, 1945

PEERS, SIR CHARLES, *Carisbrooke Castle*, HMSO, 1975

153

BIBLIOGRAPHY

PEVSNER, N. and LLOYD, D., *The Buildings of England: Hampshire and the Isle of Wight*, Penguin Books, 1967

POWELL, M., *Spithead, The Navy's Anvil*, Redan & Vedette, 1977

RIGOLD, S. E., *Yarmouth Castle*, HMSO, 1976

RULE, M., *Brading Roman Villa*, Yale University Press (London), 1974

SEYMOUR, J., *The Companion Guide to the Coast of South-East England*, Collins, 1975

SHERIDON, R. K., *Lords, Captains and Governors of the Isle of Wight*, HMSO, 1974

SIBLEY, P., *Discovering the Isle of Wight*, Robert Hale, 1977

STEERS, J. A., *The Coastline of England and Wales*, Cambridge University Press, 1946

TENNYSON, C., *Farringford, Home of Alfred Lord Tennyson*, Tennyson Research Centre, Lincoln, 1976

TOMALIN, D., *Newport Roman Villa*, Isle of Wight County Press, 1977

WHITE, A. J. OSBORNE, *A Short Account of the Geology of the Isle of Wight*, HMSO, 1921

WHITTINGTON, C. J., *Railways in the Wight*, Saunders and Co (Shanklin), 1972

WILSON, L., *Portrait of the Isle of Wight*, Robert Hale, 1965

Maps

The Solent (Sheet 196) 1:50,000 First Series, OS

Isle of Wight (Sheet 94). Reprint of the first edition of the one-inch OS of England and Wales (David & Charles, Newton Abbot).

Isle of Wight (Sheet 344, 345) Geological Survey of Great Britain

ACKNOWLEDGEMENTS

THE Isle of Wight has not lacked authors writing on the qualities of its landscape, history and general character. Of those dealing with certain aspects of the island before me, I am particularly indebted to the wealth of detailed observations and insights given by Lawrence Wilson, Pennethorne Hughes and Patricia Sibley (see bibliography). On a less descriptive level I would like to thank the many people and organisations who provided me with information on many aspects of the island. My gratitude goes to the staffs of the IOW Tourist Board (Newport), the Museum of IOW Geology (Sandown) and the IOW County Library (Newport), for their invaluable assistance and interest. I am further indebted to the local branches of The National Trust, the Young Farmers Association and the Forestry Commission, and I would also like to express my appreciation for the help received from the custodians of Carisbrooke and Yarmouth Castles, Osborne House, and to the curators of the Roman villas at Brading and Newport. Above all my appreciation goes to the island's Chief Planning Officer, Mr S. H. Greenen and his staff, who provided me with the facts on the island's economy and local problems, as summarised in Chapters 9 and 10.

On the practical side, I am indebted to Miss A. L. Laing, Mrs J. C. Simpson, Mrs M. Macleod and Mr B. Reeves, who when pressures were tense and schedules pressing, made this book possible.

Last, but certainly not least, I would like to thank Mr Lothar

ACKNOWLEDGEMENTS

Wuttke and Mr S. Robertson for the convivial evenings spent at The Bugle, Newport. Mr Wuttke was responsible for the preparation of the index.

Brian Dicks, 1979

Maps are based upon (or reproduced from) The Ordnance Survey Map with the sanction of the Controller of Her Majesty's Stationery Office. Crown Copyright Reserved. Photographs not acknowledged are from the author's collection.

INDEX

157

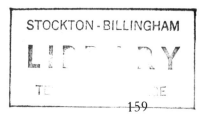